WRITING
HUMANS
AND
ROBOTS

The New Rules of Content Style

First Edition

By

Maddy Osman

Lakewood, Colorado

First edition

ISBN: 979-8-9860097-1-1

Editing by Anne Abel Smith

Editing by Stephanie Holland

Editing by Ammar Qazi

Editing by Diego Trejo

Proofreading by Kathleen Osman

PRAISE FOR

WRITING FOR
HUMANS
AND
ROBOTS

"This is *the* resource content and SEO writers desperately need. Consider it the go-to resource for how to write in a way that produces impressive SEO results without sacrificing quality!"

— Kaleigh Moore, Contributor at Forbes, Vogue Business, and Adweek and Co-Host of the Freelance Writing Coach Podcast

"The style guide on your shelf wasn't meant for the modern era. But here you've found a modern style guide, built for digital. Flip through and you'll find how different things are now. You'll see how badly this book is needed. Send a copy to a marketer on your team and they'll thank you for it."

— Andy Crestodina, Chief Marketing Officer and Co-Founder of Orbit Media Studios

"So much web content ends up in the ever-growing landfill of content that we call the internet. How do you end up standing above the noise? Maddy's *Writing for Humans and Robots: The New Rules of Content Style* prescribes a no-frills approach to web content writing that's very needed to anyone who works in the digital world."

— Bernard Huang, Co-Founder of Clearscope

"Writing content is an integral part of Search Engine Optimization. For too long, search marketers have undervalued the importance of creating content of staunch quality but with changes to Google's algorithm ignoring this skill is no longer an option. Maddy walks you through what it actually means to write well. By using concrete examples of how you should and should not construct your online content Maddy gives you a clear path toward being a better writer. All of this positions you to be able to bring in more organic traffic and more revenue."

— Mordy Oberstein, Head of SEO Branding at Wix, Advisor at Semrush, and Host of #SEOChat

"I've had the pleasure of knowing Maddy and following her work for the better part of a decade now, and her approach to creating content that actually helps people is unrivaled in the content marketing space. In an industry that's so painfully saturated with cynical tacticians just looking for a quick win and the next paycheck, I've always found Maddy's thoughtful level of care and attention to detail a welcome breath of fresh air. Her guidance on strategically balancing your writing for both human readers & the search engines of the world, is spot-on if you want to create content that'll stand the test of time."

— Ryan Robinson, Full-Time Blogger and Podcaster, Content Marketing Consultant, and Contributor to Forbes and Fast Company

"Maddy has long been my go-to for producing high-quality content people like to read, and that bots rank highly on search engines. It's a rare skill combination and she explains exactly how to do it in this book. It's a competitive advantage few would give away, and that any writer, content marketer, or person who wants their content to be found on the internet should read and implement ASAP."

— Tracey Wallace, Content Strategist at Klaviyo, formerly MarketerHire and BigCommerce

"Unlike so many books that are full of fluff, *Writing For Humans and Robots* is down to business immediately.

Within 10 minutes, I'd taken loads of notes. It was immediately clear how much we are missing from our style guide, despite building our blog for 6+ years. The book is so practical that you could copy and paste much of it into your own style guide.

I'm considering making *Writing For Humans and Robots* part of our writer onboarding. It's essentially a manual of everything you need to know to create good content, but also why those things are important.

Whether you're brand new or have been producing content for years, you'll take something away from this book that will result in better content. I'm excited for how much this is going to improve my own writing, and the consistency of content produced by our writers."

— James ("Jimmy") Rose, Co-Founder of Content Snare

"This book is legit! *Writing for Humans and Robots* is the kind of style guide I wish someone would have pointed me to when I started editing online content in 2007. Have you ever found yourself struggling with following the writing "rules"? Well, many of those rules don't apply online. And I love that Maddy calls some of those out in this book (check out Chapter 3).

Actually, now that I'm thinking about it, I'm wondering how Maddy downloaded so many of these great tips and guidelines from my brain! It's taken me nearly 20 years, writing and editing at multiple search marketing publications, to learn all of this stuff. Lucky you, you can just read this book to get the knowledge you need to start creating some fantastic content. Right now. I'll surely be pointing plenty of writers and editors toward this book."

— Danny Goodwin, Senior Editor at Search Engine Land,
formerly Executive Editor at Search Engine Journal

"Content writing for the modern age requires style. As a smart content marketer, Maddy Osman teaches respect for the reader with relevant and well-constructed copy, rather than serving forgettable lightweight fluff.

As a word lover whose goal is to make content easy to consume, she does not discriminate. Whether for humans or for robots, her style guide mindset caters to the practical and technical requirements of readership.

This book is the complete style guide for writers, marketers, and branding pros who favor substance over fluff, and who want to connect, rather than confuse. And when I say "complete," check out Maddy's appendix and resource section. Her innovative book is a seriously strong reference manual for writing better."

— Marti Konstant, Author of *Activate Your Agile Career*

"Writing for the web is becoming more complex. We're often overwhelmed by the nuances involved in writing for algorithms and the people who read our content.

Writing for Humans and Robots: The New Rules of Content Style helps you strike the balance between creating content that connects with readers and satisfies search engines. It provides a clear path through the messy process of content creation, from developing a style guide to telling stories and measuring results. Throughout, Maddy takes you through each step of her process while referencing real-world situations encountered during her time running The Blogsmith.

Maddy's writing style is energizing, and the content is straightforward with practical advice you can apply immediately. *Writing for Humans and Robots* should be required reading for any content marketing professional."

— Michael Keenan, Co-founder of Peak Freelance

"This book is making me a better writer! I've been blogging since before blogging was a word, but I've ALWAYS struggled with consistency in my formatting and writing style. Now, as a course creator, consistency is really important throughout my programs. *Writing for Humans and Robots* is helping me put together my own content style guide so that my content is consistent from blog post to blog post and program to program. Whether you're creating content alone or with a team, you need to grab your copy!"

— **Erin Flynn, Founder of Out of Office Entrepreneur**

"I've always turned to Maddy to answer all my SEO content questions. She has such a unique way of breaking down overwhelmingly complex information into simple concepts. This book is the perfect embodiment of all her expertise and skill! 10's across the board!"

— **Erika Kubick, Author of *Cheese Sex Death***

"Maddy brings to the table a vast knowledge of how content and SEO work together. *Writing for Humans and Robots* helps outline and simplify the world of content creation in a way that makes it simple and straightforward for all to understand in a thoughtful and well-constructed manner.

Nearly every company needs to create engaging content to be successful online, but it won't do any good if it can't be found. If you read this book, you'll learn how to create content that matches what your audience is looking for and can earn top visibility in organic search results.

Maddy's years of experience shine through with this guide that will help you navigate the world of writing for both humans and robots."

— **Matt Lacuesta, Director of SEO at Milestone Inc and #SEOBeers Denver Host**

"Consider *Writing for Humans and Robots* a modern-day *The Elements of Style* that picks up where most writing guidelines, like the AP Stylebook, fall short. Maddy Osman teaches online writers how to create concise, visually appealing, and compelling content for our contemporary world. I found the book to be loaded with practical style and grammar tips as well as essential online writing strategies – such as guidelines for headline writing, keyword selection, and link strategies. Maddy's writing guidelines are exactly what today's 21st-century writers have been desperately searching for and need most."

— Jenny Levine Finke, Author of *Dear Gluten, It's Not Me It's You* and Writer at goodforyouglutenfree.com

As someone who is in the habit of creating 4-5 pieces of content a week, I understand the frustration of not gaining traction, even when putting in the effort. Maddy's advice (especially on writing headlines) is incredibly valuable. I cannot recommend this book enough. It's now something I keep handy for the pieces of content I really want to make sure do well.

— Joe Casabona, Host of the How I Built It Podcast

TABLE OF CONTENTS

INTRODUCTION

How to Use This Book

Good citizens of the web care about creating content that satisfies users. However, without a fundamental set of rules to represent you and your brand, consistently pulling off content that positively impacts the user experience is close to impossible. Building up content from set guidelines is the best way to create a great content experience and raise online content quality standards.

Modern web communications are about both humans and robots. This book focuses on striking the right balance to appeal to both without compromise. While we're mostly concerned with human users, in order for them to find you, you must also consider the needs of robot search engine spiders.

This book is about creating a great experience for the reader. Regardless of who the work is for—whether you're a freelancer or brand manager—you must ultimately hold the reader in the highest regard. This means no bullshit, no useless fluff, and no expanding word count without a strategy for how it will add value.

These rules will help you create a great reader experience that also serves business goals. By standardizing the process and creating consistency, you can grow without wasting time or brainpower on unnecessary edits.

Speaking of goals, every great solution is an organic response to its creator's need to solve a problem. This book is essentially an attempt to clone myself and scale content creation, moving from freelance writer to the CEO and founder of my agency, The Blogsmith. Codifying the ideas in my head into a consistent process has allowed me to delegate high-quality content creation for the past several years. I use these concepts to produce work that I can stand behind—even if I don't ever write or edit it myself.

Selfishly, I'm writing this book because I need it to effectively explain not only *what we do* but *why we do it* as a reference for my own team. And if I'm going to put in the effort to make it a useful and exhaustive reference, I'd like to share what I know with you, too.

Although the focus of this book is primarily for writing long-form articles, many of these rules are universally relevant to a wide variety of online content formats, including social media posts, web page copy, and promotional email copy. This guide shares actionable guidance for clear and compelling communications across the various mediums online users interact with.

This style guide is broken down into three parts: writing for humans, writing for robots, and how to put it all together into a content creation process. Inevitably, there is some intermixing between each section—especially as artificial intelligence (AI) and machine learning bring robot understanding closer to human reality. But ultimately, the most important users are the humans, and brands should focus primarily on appealing to them.

This book is also broken down by concept so you can jump around for guidance relating to whatever part of the process you're currently focusing on, such as fact-checking claims, consulting proper grammar for different situations, or determining ideal word choice. In each section, there are examples to help you apply the concepts.

In addition to this in-depth guide, you'll have the opportunity to access a short-form version of The Blogsmith Style Guide for quick reference (without all the extra context). Access details are located in the Appendix.

Your style guide and mine may look a lot different—and that's encouraged.

Like learning a foreign language to strengthen your native language skills, immersing yourself in the style guide for another brand or medium can likewise be a useful exercise. Understanding a specific brand's unique voice, tone, products, and customers (and other important details) requires a deep dive of its own, but these guidelines serve true regardless of who you're writing for. Diving into the details gets your gears turning and ultimately results in better content.

The guidance I've shared is based on the experiences I've had while creating high-performing content, mixed with AP news style guidelines that clarify the ideal end result. When you're not sure what to do, *The Associated Press (AP) Stylebook* is a useful fallback when you haven't otherwise specified a brand-specific rule.

And who am I to be making suggestions for proper style?

- I'm the daughter of an English teacher mom. Needless to say, I was mercilessly corrected for every improper "my friend and me are going to. . ." uttered in willful ignorance. I'm also the daughter of an entrepreneur dad who taught me how to run a successful business by following proper process.
- I'm a lifelong book nerd who always completed the library summer reading challenge as a young student. In 2019, I set and achieved the goal of reading 100 books. I'm an active book club member. I love discovering words I didn't know and savoring an exceptional turn of phrase.
- Finally, I've been running a profitable content writing business for over eight years with plentiful experience managing a content team and acting as the editor-in-chief for all the brands we serve. The Blogsmith Style Guide is based on eight years of improving my editing process, then codifying it for others to follow (and expand on) to achieve consistent results.

This book isn't gospel. It's a set of rules that have served The Blogsmith well. It's a protocol developed by working with dozens of tough editors over many years—from brands across the spectrum of B2B (business-to-business) offerings, with a few fun B2C (business-to-consumer) clients thrown in the mix. It involves the many realizations I've had about what works, including takeaways from my best-performing content with tens of thousands of reads.

And these ideas aren't exactly novel. You probably follow many of these principles automatically after working with the tough editors in your life. Their usefulness lies in their potential for consistency. This book provides concrete instructions and use cases to otherwise abstract thoughts about something not sounding or looking quite right.

This is a book of rules that work for many top brands online. Take the time to understand them and why they've been shared here. Then, if you can think of a better way of doing things—break the rules.

Happy writing!

Maddy Osman, Founder of The Blogsmith

P.S. Like other style guides, nothing here should be considered final. When enough of these rules change, it will be time for a new edition. If you have any suggestions for future editions of this book, share your thoughts with **style@theblogsmith.com**.

All resources mentioned throughout the book are cited in the Bibliography or Appendix.

Find bonus resources for this book at

www.writingforhumansandrobots.com/bonuses.

To me style is just the outside of content, and content the inside of style, like the outside and the inside of the human body—both go together, they can't be separated.

—Jean-Luc Godard

PART 1

WRITING FOR HUMANS

 Chapter 1

Important Considerations
When Choosing Words

If you commit nothing else from this guide to memory, at least commit to internalizing this:

Words matter.

Words can inspire—or they can alienate. Using certain words can be polarizing. As such, you must be thoughtful when choosing words to describe specific things and situations. After all, nuance helps to convey meaning. Your word choice may have different effects depending on the audience.

That being said, here are some guidelines you can use to create a level of consistency around voice as it's conveyed by word choice.

Voice/Tone Spectrum

The Nielsen Norman Group helps simplify the process of codifying voice and tone with these four dimensions:

1. Funny versus serious.
2. Formal versus casual.
3. Respectful versus irreverent.
4. Enthusiastic versus matter-of-fact.[1]

Start with agreement on these basics before writing for a new brand.

---

[1] Kate Moran, "The Four Dimensions of Tone of Voice," Nielsen Norman Group, 2016, https://www.nngroup.com/articles/tone-of-voice-dimensions/.

Writing with Concise, Simple Language

Complicated, multisyllabic words are not preferred by internet readers. Their objective is to locate information rapidly, and dense content is not the territory in which to navigate. Your competition has likely realized this, and your audience may default to them if you're not meeting them halfway with simple language.

As such, here are some guidelines for writing with simple language:

Say more with less. **Cut unnecessary words**. Aim for "concise."

For example:

Instead of *"more and more,"* just go with *"more."*

Besides complex industry-specific words that you can't avoid without losing meaning, **use uncomplicated language**. Assume middle-school level reading comprehension. Consider writing at a reading level below what you normally expect for complex topics.

Don't repeat the same words too close together in the same sentence or paragraph. It comes across as lazy and uninspired. Vary your word choice.

Cut out fluff words. These are words that don't add value or can be removed without changing meaning.

For example:

- *"That"*—Instead of *"They say **that** it's better,"* choose *"They say it's better."*
- *"Simply"* or *"Just"*—Instead of *"**Simply** open the app,"* choose *"Open the app."*
- *"However"* and *"So"*—These words **can** be useful but are often unnecessary. Ask yourself if you need the word or if your sentence makes sense without it.

Choose strong verbs instead of adverbs. Rather than modifying a common verb or adjective, choose a less common option that better conveys your intention in a stronger, single word.

For example:

Don't write this:
"We're very excited."

Write this instead:
"We're thrilled."

A Reminder about Possessives

Sometimes, it's nice to restate existing grammar rules that have a knack for getting confused.

Here are the guidelines about possessives for writers in The Blogsmith Style Guide:

If the word is plural and ends in an "s," put the apostrophe at the end.

For example:

"Those classes' schedules."

If the word is singular and ends in an "s," add an apostrophe and an additional "s."

For example:

"That class's schedule."

Making References to People or Objects

Clarify your ideas by making appropriate references in your writing.

If you're referring to a brand, restate the brand name in every paragraph in which it's mentioned (don't refer to the brand as "it").

Pro tip:

While going through edits, repeat the proper noun/noun of whatever you're referring to, determining whether it sounds weird in a sentence out of context.

For example:

A sentence like, "*It is useful for all e-commerce niches,*" doesn't make as much sense out of context as "*WooCommerce is useful for all e-commerce niches.*"

If you're referring to a company, it is a thing rather than a person.

For example:

Don't write this:
"*the company **who**.*"

Write this instead:
"*the company **that**.*"

Always choose positive language when referring to the brand commissioning the content. Avoid phrasing that could be interpreted negatively, even in subtle or unintended ways. Spin limitations positively.

For example:

Don't write this:
"*Previously only available in the US.*"

Write this instead:
"*Available in the US at launch.*"

Avoiding Ambiguity

On a related note, **don't leave room for ambiguity** when referencing different concepts. Take this opportunity to add clarity with a related search engine optimization (SEO) keyword, if possible.

For example:

Instead of a sentence ending in "it," such as *"How do you do—?,"* fill in the blank. **What is *it*?**

Here are some additional examples of ambiguity and what to do instead:

- *"Many"* is less clear than *"50%"* or even *"the majority."* If you say, *"Many people love this product,"* take the opportunity to prove it by quoting positive customer reviews.
- When you use a number, tell the reader *how many of **what*** (offer a specific unit of measurement).
- Instead of saying, *"See how things are going,"* be specific about what the *"things"* are.

Finally, when making any comparison, be clear about what you're comparing something to.

For example:

In addition to:	Add:
"Most e-commerce businesses have to process much more data through their website"	*"than a standard business website."*

This is a little nitpicky, but in headings, The Blogsmith uses **"advantages and disadvantages"** rather than "pros and cons." It sounds more like a complete thought.

Using Inclusive Language

Why bother with inclusive language? Because we never want someone to feel left out, like their needs are a burden, or you're judging them for something they can't control. Using inclusive language is a good way to show your audience that you care about everyone's preferences, not just those of one specific group. Depending on your target market, you can adjust the exact nature of the inclusivity of your content.

Default to gender-neutral language. Instead of generalizing with **his or her** or **she or he**, use "their" or "they."

If you're writing for a brand and the article is going on their website, don't refer to the brand in the third person. It should be a first-person plural when the client is referring to themselves in an article.

For example:

Don't write this:	Write this instead:
"The company"	*"Our company," "we," "us"*

Here are some further guidelines for ensuring inclusivity:

- Use people-first language that doesn't put weight on descriptors over characteristics. For example, you might refer to someone with a hearing disability as "a person who is deaf" instead of "a deaf person."
- Use approachable language that doesn't unintentionally alienate—learn more about the nuances around word choice in Chapter 2.

Here are some words to avoid and to use instead:

- Instead of "old," try "aging/older."
- Instead of "girlfriend" or "boyfriend," try "partner."
- Instead of "homeless," try "person experiencing homelessness."
- Instead of "accused," try "reported."

Words and Phrases to Avoid Completely

Some words shouldn't be used when creating online content because they're either confusing or devoid of real value.

These guidelines will keep you on the right track for creating quality content that doesn't mince words:

Don't use -ing suffixes together.

For example:

"Involving throwing" should be *"that involved throwing."*

Don't use "ones" to describe a noun you've already defined. Use the same word again or find another way to say it.

For example:

"During the interview process, be sure to ask the right questions. This could be a mix of common restaurant job interview questions and ~~ones~~ (try **"those"***) that are more unique to your company's culture."*

Here are some word choice swaps you can make to improve your writing:

- "Utilize"—choose "use."
- "Aside from"—choose "besides."
- "Host"—choose "a variety," "a number of," or "suite."
- "Allow"—choose something less passive, like "empower" or "enable."
- "Cheap"—choose variations of "affordable."

Also, remove "thankfully," "fortunately," "luckily," or "actually," and any other words that don't add value. Instead of these terms, try a bucket brigade like "**Here's the good news:**."

But what is a bucket brigade? This is defined in <ins>Chapter 4</ins>, with more examples.

Avoid using words that might insult the reader's intelligence. We're trying to educate people, so don't assume anything is obvious. Avoid phrases like "obviously," "of course," "clearly," and "everyone knows."

Instead of "COVID-19," use "the pandemic." When it comes to search engines and social media platforms, ranking COVID-19 content is reserved for relevant authorities sharing public health information. Confusing the algorithm by including similar phrases in your less-relevant content may jeopardize the ranking of your articles that aren't about public health information.

Even after the pandemic is over, it's important not to optimize for keywords people use to locate health and safety information. When talking about an adjacent (but not as critical) topic, use a thesaurus to come up with alternate labels.

 **Chapter 2**

General Style Guidelines

Regardless of your content's medium, many style rules apply no matter what.

Keep the following rules in mind for any project, adapting them to your specific branding rules.

Sentence Structure

Let's start with the basics: how to write sentences.

Start by specifying a word count average or range for the content piece. At The Blogsmith, unless otherwise noted, articles are a **minimum of 1,000 words**. The average articles we create are between 1,000 and 1,500 words.

- **Don't bury the lede**. The direction of the sentence should be made clear as soon as possible—so the reader isn't forced to read it all the way through to make sense of it.

For example:

Don't write this:	Write this instead:
"There's a new way to accept payments, specifically for e-commerce and your WordPress website. If you use WooCommerce, you can benefit from WooCommerce payments. It's just launched in 5 new countries."	*"WooCommerce Payments, an integrated payment solution for WooCommerce stores, is now available in five new countries. It can now be used by WooCommerce stores across Great Britain, Ireland, Australia, New Zealand, and Canada."*

Avoid the obvious and make the reader's job as easy as possible by supplying quality information. If it doesn't add value—cut it.

For example:

Don't write this:	Write this instead:
"Please allow me to tell you all about watercolor painting. You're going to need a bunch of specialized supplies. It's going to take some time to learn. Art is so cool, right?"	*"Watercolor is a specific form of painting that combines special pigments with water for unique, organic effects. To get started, you'll want watercolor paper, paints, a few basic watercolor brushes, and a palette for mixing colors and intensities. Don't get overwhelmed before giving it a try—you can learn to create beautiful watercolor paintings in just one sitting."*

If one sentence can be split into two, do it. Shorter sentences are less likely to be misunderstood. Sentences that run on can be confusing.

For example:

Don't write this:	Write this instead:
"The primary call to action (ideally, there isn't more than one—that confuses people and makes it harder for them to make a decision) needs to be repeated strategically, multiple times throughout the page."	*"There should be just one main call to action (CTA), repeated strategically, multiple times throughout the page. Multiple CTAs confuse people and make it harder for them to make a decision."*

Abbreviations

Yes, even the way you abbreviate words should follow some level of consistency.

If you're defining something as a plural (e.g., calls to action), **make sure the abbreviation is also plural** (e.g., CTAs).

Avoid cutesy abbreviations: For example, "veggies" should be "vegetables."

When using an abbreviation (e.g., "CTA"), make sure to **define it the first time you use it** in an article (e.g., "call to action (CTA)"). Then use the abbreviation alone thereafter.

Punctuation

Basic grammar rules are your fallback to determining proper punctuation for web content. But you may want to detail brand-specific rules (if different than your reference style guide), such as whether you're for or against em-dashes (—).

The Blogsmith has two all-encompassing rules for punctuation style:

- **Avoid using exclamation marks** unless absolutely necessary.
- Use the **Oxford comma** (also known as the "serial comma": item 1, item 2, and item 3) so your meaning is not unintentionally confused.

Constructing Ideas with Text

Once you've figured out the basics of style, it's worth spending time developing a clear voice.

Here are some ideas for constructing and effectively communicating ideas through text:

Generally, it's a good idea to **avoid absolutes**. Nothing is "perfect," and, usually, there are at least a few (likely obvious) exceptions to every rule.

- **Avoid clichés** and popular sayings—find a different way to say what you mean to say.
  Clichés are trite and, quite frankly, lazy. Using them means taking a shortcut while trying to communicate what you *really* mean. They're used so often that they don't really mean

anything. You're better off using concise language to get your message across.

Perhaps the only time you'd want to use a cliché is to emphasize a point, such as when you're trying to tell a story. Here are some common clichés to keep on your radar in an effort to avoid them, plus some alternative ways to say what you mean:

- "Word to the wise"—"here's what you need to know."
- "Can of worms"—"problem."
- "Day in, day out"—"every day."
- "Get your feet wet"—"try."
- "I beg to differ"—"I disagree."
- "Like clockwork"—"a habit."
- "Needless to say"—"that said."
- "Plain as day"—"clear."
- "Scared to death"—"terrified."
- "Time is of the essence"—"there's a looming deadline."
- "Wet behind the ears"—"inexperienced."

- **Never make assumptions about someone's knowledge of a topic**, even if something seems obvious to a certain target audience. **Err on the side of over-explaining**.

- **Don't start articles with a definition**. Too many articles on the internet start with a heading such as, *"What is [topic]?"* or *"What [topic] is."* Starting an article this way makes your content sound unoriginal and formulaic. Even when writing an informational article, find a different way to present an explanation of the concept.

   If you're creating a featured snippet (see Chapter 12), place it further down in the article. Most of the time, you can define the article's key term in the introductory paragraphs before you create your first subheading.

Alternative headings that you can use to incorporate a definition of the key term are:

- *"How ___ Works"*
- *"Basics of ___"*
- *"Why ___ Is Crucial"*
- *"___ 101"*

This rule doesn't apply to keywords in headings. The exception to that rule is when optimizing for keywords in headings. For example, if you're optimizing for *"what is a website builder?,"* you can use that keyword as a heading.

Providing a Great Reader Experience

Creating high-quality content in the digital age means satisfying the needs of human readers while optimizing for the basics of the search engine spiders.

Here are some guidelines for creating content that people will find worth reading and recommending:

- **Avoid ending sentences with** "**etc.**": Instead, just add the word "and" before the last list item and start the list with the word "including." The word "including" implies that there are more options and given items are just a few examples.
- **Don't use the passive voice**: Opt for the active voice.

For example:

Don't write this:	Write this instead:
"Metaverse was launched by Mark Zuckerberg in 2021."	*"Mark Zuckerberg launched Metaverse in 2021."*

Writing in the active voice results in concise, yet energetic, content. A premium grammar-checking tool like Grammarly can send prompts if you use the passive voice, as well as give tips for turning a sentence into the active voice.

- **Write with conviction**: If you make a claim, don't cast doubt or downplay it by using words such as "likely" or "maybe." Own what you're writing, or don't write it at all.

- **If you give information in one part of an article, don't contradict it in another**. Similarly, if you make an *absolute claim*, don't talk about *exceptions to your claim* later in the same article.

For example:

Don't make this claim in body text: "*Every business must get an Employer Identification Number (EIN)*"	And then, later in the article, include the heading: "*Types of Businesses That Don't Need an Employer Identification Number*"

- **Don't break the "4th wall": avoid referring to the article itself**. Avoid saying "in this article" or "in this post." It's awkward, and it interrupts the reader's flow.

  But if you're writing in-depth about a certain topic or process, you can use the word "guide" to refer to it because this distinction is less about the medium and more about describing the content's purpose.

For example:

Don't write this: "*In this post, I'll tell you about: [list]*"	Write this instead: "*In this guide, we'll go through: [list]*"

Perspective

Getting the perspective right is mostly about consistency. But make sure you have guidance on whether to default to the first-, second-, or third-person. For starters, using the active voice instead of the passive can help you clarify the perspective.

For example:

Don't write this:	Write this instead:
"It should be done [x] way."	*"You should do it [x] way."*

At The Blogsmith, the default guideline is to write in the **second-person**: "you" not "I," "me," or "they" unless otherwise instructed. The obvious exception would be an article about someone's first-hand experience they intend to share from their personal perspective.

Also, don't forget **Yooto: You only own things once**. Taking out "you/your" words can simplify a sentence.

For example:

Don't write this:	Write this instead:
"You can tweak your card settings to lock out your chosen company expenses."	*"You can tweak the card settings to lock out certain company expenses."*

Writing the Conclusion

Finish strong with a solid conclusion.

End the article with a relevant call to action—for example, to comment, get in touch, or tweet at @*[brand]*'s Twitter handle.

Use the end of an article to **draw the topic back to the brand** and bring together all the content in a relevant way.

 **Chapter 3**

Grammar Rules to Break on the Web

It's important to learn the rules of grammar before attempting to break them.

Spending time doing this will give you a solid understanding of the "why" behind the existence of these rules. It will also help you determine whether any grammar-checking tools you're using, like Grammarly, really have authority when making suggestions for improving your content.

As language evolves, certain words that start out spelled one way may one day be accepted with the "incorrect" spelling. But just as the grammatically correct way of expressing things doesn't always mesh with society's contextual development over time, the same can be said when adapting commonly accepted grammar rules for print on the web.

Creating content for the web means that you're publishing to a medium that has the capacity to change rapidly. Unlike with printed books or periodical publications, you can make edits after something has already been shared publicly. As such, the bar for formality is a lot lower on the web than with print media.

What usually matters when it comes to formal writing is a lot less important when it comes to web writing. So, drown out that English teacher's voice in your head. You can make the following adaptations when creating web content without worrying about being "incorrect."

Ending a Sentence with a Preposition

In general, when it comes to writing for the web and dealing with grammar, a **conversational** style is better than a strict interpretation of the "rules." As such, the standard rule of not ending a sentence with a preposition is one that needs to be relaxed.

According to Merriam-Webster, the original purpose of this rule was to align the English language with Latin, which syntactically didn't allow for prepositions at the end of a sentence.[2] But when it comes to news writing, which characterizes most blog-style web content, *The Associated Press (AP) Stylebook* sanctions the use of a preposition at the end of a sentence.[3]

In this case, go ahead and write in a conversational tone without fear of losing meaning or coming across as someone who doesn't proofread their work.

What are you waiting for?

Beginning a Sentence with "And," "Or," "But"

As with the previous grammar rule of not ending a sentence with a preposition, web content style has also relaxed the long-held belief that you should never begin a sentence with coordinating conjunctions such as "and," "or," "but."

There's nothing in the *AP Stylebook* that suggests avoiding conjunctions at the beginning of a sentence. And according to *The Chicago Manual of Style*, "a substantial percentage (often as many as 10 percent) of the sentences in first-rate writing begin with conjunctions."[4]

---

[2] "Prepositions, Ending a Sentence With," Merriam-Webster, 2019, https://www.merriam-webster.com/words-at-play/prepositions-ending-a-sentence-with.

[3] "Ask the Editor: Should a Sentence End with a Preposition?" Associated Press Stylebook, accessed March 7, 2022, https://www.apstylebook.com/ask_the_editors/41877.

[4] University of Chicago Press, *The Chicago Manual of Style*, 16th ed. (Chicago: University of Chicago Press, 2010).

All that said, according to *AP Stylebook* editors, the key to proper use is *moderation*.[5] Remember that the true purpose of coordinating conjunctions is to create a connection between two ideas. If you're not using coordinating conjunctions to make connections between different sentences within your content, you're missing the point.

And wouldn't that be a shame?

Avoiding Contractions

As with almost every grammar "rule" discussed here, the rules for formal writing and writing for the web digress when it comes to contractions.

With readability in mind, create content in the way you'd talk naturally. There's no need to spell out "will not" when "won't" captures the nuance more succinctly.

If you're still wondering about any "official" rulings on this aspect of grammar, the *AP Stylebook* supports the use of common contractions.[6]

Won't you give contractions a try?

Avoiding the Use of Personal Pronouns ("I," "Me," etc.)

When I first started freelance writing, editors insisted that a first-person perspective was not considered ideal. As I gained more experience and clients wanted to share that perspective in their content, it was hard to overcome the memory of past edits.

So which perspective is technically considered correct?

Ultimately, it comes down to the nature of the content you're creating.

---

[5] "Ask the Editor: Beginning a Sentence with a Conjunction.," Associated Press Stylebook, accessed March 7, 2022, https://www.apstylebook.com/ask_the_editors/25415.
[6] "AP Stylebook: Contractions," Associated Press Stylebook, accessed March 7, 2022, https://www.apstylebook.com/ap_stylebook/contractions.

When you're creating content about someone's experience, it should be written from that person's perspective: first-person if you're the writer (or ghostwriter) and you're sharing a personal experience, and third-person if you're writing about someone else's experience. An example of first-person is how I shared my own experience about using perspective in writing in the first paragraph of this section..

	Singular	Plural
1st person	I, me	we, us
2nd person	you	you
3rd person	they, them	them

Figure 3.1 Pronoun perspective chart: 1st, 2nd, 3rd person singular and plural.

If you're writing more generally about a topic, the second person ("you") is preferred because it directly addresses the reader, engaging with them and drawing them into the content.

At any rate, there's no perspective that's "wrong," but, again, it should be driven by the topic and the origin of your information. That said, in general, it's hard for other people to connect with your writing if it's only about you ("I") without inviting them in ("you").

While you should keep your perspective consistent throughout a given piece of writing, make sure your personal pronoun use isn't unintentionally alienating your audience.

Avoiding Short Paragraphs

Grammarly cites common educator guidance for writing paragraphs as 100–200 words or 5–6 sentences.[7] When it comes to formal writing or printed materials, this guidance largely holds true as a rule. But when it comes to writing for the web, shorter sentences and paragraphs are much easier to read.

---

[7] "How Long Is a Paragraph?" Grammarly, April 6, 2017, https://www.grammarly.com/blog/how-long-is-a-paragraph/.

Think about it this way:

Whether you're skimming an article on a laptop or trying to read something on your phone, coming across a huge wall of text makes the experience frustrating—to the point where you may **bounce** from the website (leave without visiting any other pages) in search of a more abbreviated answer elsewhere. And, more than likely, a fix is a simple matter of the writer splitting up the same sentences into additional paragraphs to create a better reading experience.

In any case, incorporating white space with shorter sentences and paragraphs (in addition to the use of ordered and unordered lists— see Chapter 6) will create a better reading experience for your audience. Simplify sentences that run on in a way that's hard to follow. With that in mind, aim for 2–3 sentences within a paragraph and sentences that don't exceed two lines.

That said, you *could* go even shorter with one-sentence paragraphs — which are great for creating emphasis.

Speaking of creating emphasis...

Avoiding Sentence Fragments

A sentence fragment is something that may look and feel like a sentence but isn't technically one.

Here's why:

- It may lack a subject: *"Running in the fields"* or a verb: *"Too much work."*
- It may be a dependent clause: *"As a freelance editor who manages content for engineering companies."*

As such, fragments are grammatically incorrect.

But as you've likely picked up by now, many strict grammar rules were meant to be broken when it comes to writing for the web. Or even for print, as Aldous Huxley demonstrates in this example from *Brave New*

World:

> *"A squat grey building of only thirty-four stories. Over the main entrance the words CENTRAL LONDON HATCHERY AND CONDITIONING CENTRE, and, in a shield, the World State's motto, COMMUNITY, IDENTITY, STABILITY."*[8]

The key is to use sentence fragments with purpose. Great authors employ sentence fragments to add emphasis that will help get their ideas across. They clear up any confusion created by a fragment with full sentences immediately following or preceding the sentence fragments.

Don't Use Slang

This grammar rule is made to be broken because the nature of your audience should decide your specific word choice—not some outdated grammar guide.

That said, and as with most of the grammar rules discussed here, don't overdo it. Use slang *sparingly* so as not to distract the reader from the meaning behind the content you're creating. Also, don't force the use of a word that you think would be "cool" to your audience if you don't really understand the word and its correct context.

---

[8] Aldous Huxley, *Brave New World* (United Kingdom: Chatto & Windus, 1932).

Figure 3.2 A great meme about unsuccessfully trying to relate to kids.[9]

A better and more helpful rule for creating great web content is to avoid using *jargon*. And whenever you must use a word that's unique to your industry, make sure to define it at its first mention. As with big, complicated words, insider jargon only alienates your audience unless you add context. The same goes for abbreviations and acronyms—define them early on and then subsequently use the short form (see Chapter 2).

In general, assume only a baseline of understanding when it comes to industry jargon and seek out simpler terms whenever possible.

The Bottom Line

When writing for the web, ignore the most restrictive rules of formal writing.

As a very general rule, if it sounds good out loud, as in a conversation, it's likely fair game for web content writing.

The Flesch Reading Ease test measures the average length of sentences (based on word count) and the average number of syllables in the words you choose. The higher the score, the easier it

---

[9] John Riggi, "The Tuxedo Begins," *30 Rock* (NBC, February 16, 2012).

is to read your content.[10]

Contrary to popular belief, Google doesn't consider readability scores while indexing content.[11] However, readability could improve your conversion rates.[12]

$$RE = 206.835 - (1.015 \times ASL) - (84.6 \times ASW)$$

RE = Readability Ease   **ASL = Average Sentence Length**

ASW = Average number of syllables per word

Figure 3.3 Calculation to determine Flesch Reading Ease.

Part of achieving ideal readability is writing for people with a low average reading level. As a rule of thumb, aim to write for an eighth-grade reading level. But that's not a hard and fast rule—you can adjust this metric based on your ideal target reader.

In general, many formal writing rules can get in the way of easy readability—which can have snowballing negative impacts on your content efforts. So, before throwing in a $5 word to stoke your own ego, consider if it's truly adding value for your ideal target reader. After all, it's not about whether *you* like the content but whether *your audience* will.

---

[10] "The Flesch Reading Ease Score: Why and How to Use It," *Yoast* (blog), May 20, 2019, https://yoast.com/flesch-reading-ease-score/.

[11] Travis Mcknight, "Study: How Content Readability Affects SEO and Rankings," Portent, June 17, 2021, https://www.portent.com/blog/content/study-how-content-readability-affects-seo-and-rankings.htm.

[12] Jackie Jeffers, "Study: The Readability of Your Website Is Affecting Your Conversion Rates," Portent, November 17, 2020, https://www.portent.com/blog/cro/study-the-readability-of-your-website-is-affecting-your-conversion-rates.htm.

 **Chapter 4**

How to Improve Web Content Readability with Formatted Text

The fundamental rules of great copywriting hold true, regardless of the medium. That said, some of the biggest differences between types of output (book, manual, ad copy, etc.) are the specific formatting rules you need to keep in mind to convey your message effectively.

Writing for the web involves balancing the needs of a human reader with the technical requirements of a search engine spider. And for both perspectives, online content creation requires optimizing for a short attention span.

Great formatting will help improve readability for humans, providing an enjoyable user experience that will help retain visitors and build brand equity for your organization or product.

The human approach also plays well with search engine algorithms. Google's 2019 BERT (Bidirectional Encoder Representations from Transformers) algorithm update considerably reduced old requirements for exact match keywords, so create content that reads naturally to future-proof its quality.[13]

Algorithms will continue to evolve and become more sophisticated. In that sense, you no longer have to sacrifice quality for machine readability—optimize for the human.

---

[13] Pandu Nayak, "Understanding Searches Better than Ever Before," Google, October 25, 2019, https://blog.google/products/search/search-language-understanding-bert/.

Parallelism

Be consistent. If you start a list and end one point with a period, make sure all list items reflect the same style.

This is also known as **parallelism**.

For example:

- **Step 1**: Log in to the WordPress dashboard.
- **Step 2**: Navigate to the **Settings** screen.
- **Step 3**: Click on **Reading**.

There are six instances of parallelism in the example above:

- The label for each step always has **bold** formatting.
- Each step is labeled to show that it's part of the same sequence (Step 1, Step 2, etc.) and is followed by a colon.
- Specific user interface elements, which the reader is instructed to interact with, also have **bold** formatting.
- The word following the step number is an action verb.
- The text after the colon is capitalized.
- Each bullet point ends with a period.

Put simply, all elements in a list should follow the same style to achieve consistency.

This includes capitalization—an issue that often comes up in edits. If you capitalize one type of element, you need to capitalize all other types of that element. Punctuation must also be consistent across elements. Paying attention to these details is important for respecting and applying a brand's preferred formatting.

Pro tip:

Ask yourself: is all punctuation within quotation marks?

Another point to consider is whether consistency in punctuation should also apply to subheadings.

For example:

If you're writing a **listicle**, make sure the subheadings for each list item are numbered:

1. *[First Item Name]*
2. *[Second Item Name]*
3. *[Third Item Name]*

When it comes to numbered subheadings, a personal preference is that no item in the ordered list should be indented.

For example:

Don't write this:
[Indent] 1. [Item Name]

Write this instead:
1. [Item Name] (no indent)

Pro tip:

To prevent auto-formatting a subheading as an ordered list with indentations, first, input the number, then press the spacebar, and finally type in the period that follows the list item number. Delete the space, then finish by writing the item name. Depending on your word processor, the text may auto-format with an indent that's hard to adjust if you don't follow these directions.

When creating your own style guide, you may also have opinions about spacing around an **ellipsis** (. . .) and whether or not to use an **em-dash** (—) (or both). It may also make sense to set a style guide rule about limiting the frequency of em-dashes next to each other, plus any repetitive formatting that leads to compound sentences. Repetition can be perceived as sloppiness.

For example:

With multiple em-dashes:	Without multiple em-dashes:
"By combining Leadfeeder—which empowers you to see which companies visited your site—and the Sales Navigator—which also shows you contacts from within the company—you can conduct more specific targeting."	*"By combining Leadfeeder (which empowers you to see which companies visited your site) and the Sales Navigator (which also shows you contacts from within the company), you can conduct more specific targeting."*

Also, limit the frequency of commas next to each other.

For example:

Don't write this:	Write this instead:
"He listed the qualities, like intelligence, humor, conservatism, and independence, that he liked in an executive."	*"He listed the qualities— intelligence, humor, conservatism, independence—that he liked in an executive."*

Here's a more general final note on parallelism, one regarding etiquette more than style: when creating content for the web, make sure all typography and styling for subsection elements remain consistent.

It's sloppy to deliver a draft that doesn't retain standard formatting.

White Space

Google Search Quality Rater Guidelines are used to audit and improve search results quality via human Quality Raters.[14] For web content creators, these guidelines are a useful resource that hints at the various content formatting elements that make up a high Page Quality score.

---

[14] Google, "Search Quality Rater Guidelines" (Google, October 19, 2021), https://static.googleusercontent.com/media/guidelines.raterhub.com/en//searchqualityevaluator guidelines.pdf.

A recurring theme across the guidelines is that walls of text and visual clutter make for a poor reading experience. As such, it's crucial to incorporate white space to make it easier for users to find the specific answers they're searching for.

The Quality Rater Guidelines were designed to service users who want to find answers to their questions quickly and easily. In many cases, users expect their query to be resolved within Google's own search engine results pages (SERPs)—without clicking through to another website.

A **SERP** is the page you see after typing your search query and hitting "enter." It displays paid ads, the top organic search results, and other relevant Google features (like Google Maps results).

White space can help create a frustration-free user experience because it results in a less overwhelming environment in which to find answers.

But how do you promote a consistent standard for incorporating white space? You can't. You *should* allow for some natural variation. But, in general, as previously mentioned in Chapter 2, stick to short sentences and paragraphs to increase white space.

Adding Emphasis

High-quality online content is optimized for short attention spans. As such, you should use formatting to draw attention to certain elements or to help convey meaning.

Here are some specific guidelines established at The Blogsmith:

Text Decorations

Use text decorations (**bold**, *italics*, underline, etc.) to draw attention to stand-out facts within your articles.

For example:

"Text messages are <u>not</u> more secure than emails."

If you use a text-decoration, don't extend the formatting to punctuation such as colons, periods, and commas.

For example:

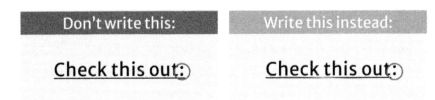

Figure 4.1 An example of careful formatting with text decorations and punctuation.

Add **bold** formatting to any word, phrase, acronym, or concept when you define it.

For example:

*"**A/B testing** involves evaluating the conversion effectiveness of two different versions of an element."*

When referring to user interface (UI) elements, such as a menu or tab in the WordPress dashboard, use **bold** formatting for mentions of UI elements—but not the generic labels that describe them (*"menu"*, *"tab"*).

Don't use quotation marks in place of **bold** formatting when referring to UI elements.

For example:

*"In your WordPress dashboard, click on **WooCommerce > Settings > Shipping tab > Leave At Door.**"*

Use **bold** formatting, rather than quotation marks, for the titles of a company's proprietary offerings.

For example:

*"Instagram offers immersive experiences through **Collections**."*

Avoid Excessive Formatting

Emphasis can also be taken away with poor formatting. Excessive parentheses are an example of this point. Use them sparingly because they can detract from the main point. If the text in parentheses is closer to a full sentence in length, turn it into a sentence instead.

For example:

Don't write this:	Write this instead:
"I'm a Broncos fan (but I really don't care about football)."	*"I'm a Broncos fan. But I really don't care about football."*

Bucket Brigades

Use bucket brigades and add white space whenever possible to keep people reading.[15]

Bucket brigades involve the use of a brief phrase, followed by a colon or question mark. They help introduce useful white space variation between long paragraphs while also re-engaging the reader.

Here are some bucket brigade examples:

- *"Here's the deal:"*
- *"Now:"*
- *"What's the bottom line?"*
- *"You might be wondering:"*

---

[15] Joanna Wiebe, "How to Engage with the Bucket Brigade Technique," Copyhackers, October 3, 2017, https://copyhackers.com/engage-bucket-brigade-technique/.

- *"This is wild:"*
- *"It gets better/worse:"*
- *"But here's the kicker:"*
- *"Want to know the best part?"*

Capitalizations

The most important style rule to hold dear when it comes to capitalization is what Dale Carnegie famously wrote in his book *How to Win Friends and Influence People*:

"A person's name is to that person the. . . most important sound in any language."[16]

On a related note, the correct capitalization and spacing of a brand's name are important to the brands you write for and about, so double-check that you have them right.

A great way to check for correct capitalization (also spacing between words) is to reference the brand's website, footer text, and social media accounts.

For example:

- It's *"WordPress"*—not *"Wordpress."*
- It's *"HubSpot"*—not *"Hubspot."*
- It's *"Mailchimp"*—not *"MailChimp."*

The Blogsmith Style Guide also instructs writers to follow this rule when referring to a URL (WordPress.com not Wordpress.com).

---

[16] Dale Carnegie, *How to Win Friends and Influence People* (United States: Simon & Schuster, 1936).

Chapter 5

Formatting Numbers in Written Content

One of the simplest ways to get people interested in your content is by quantifying the various claims you make. But as with every other major aspect of style, there are rules and consistencies to keep in mind if high-quality content is your goal.

For the most part, The Blogsmith Style Guide defers to Associated Press (AP) style. You can use standards like the *AP Stylebook* as a reference frame to develop your own guidelines.

The first and most important rule for using numbers is to **avoid ambiguity**. If you write a number, make sure you define the specific thing you're numbering, even if it is already implied.

For example:

Don't write this:	Write this instead:
"The limit is 300."	*"The limit is 300 emails."*

When writing dates, abbreviate the month for a specific date. Per AP style, don't abbreviate March, April, June, and July.[17]

For example:

"Nov. 26, 2020."

Spell out the month when referring to just a month and year.

---

[17] "AP Stylebook: Months," Associated Press Stylebook, accessed March 17, 2022, https://www.apstylebook.com/ap_stylebook/months.

For example:

"November 2020."

Using Symbols

Clarify how writers should incorporate (or avoid) symbols.

When writing about money, use numbers and a relevant currency symbol (like a dollar sign).

For example:

"$6," "$1 million."

For cents, spell out the word.

For example:

"5 cents."

AP style uses the % symbol for percentages when paired with a number mid-sentence. In other words, you must spell out the number and the word "percent" when it's referenced at the beginning of a sentence.[18] But as with em-dash styling, some brands are particular about their approach around percentage styling—opting to spell out the word "percent" in every instance instead of using the symbol. If there's a preference either way, make sure it's documented.

---

[18] "AP Stylebook: Percent, Percentage, Percentage Points," Associated Press Stylebook, accessed March 17, 2022, https://www.apstylebook.com/ap_stylebook/percent-percentage-percentage-points.

When to Use Numbers versus Words

Let writers know when to use numbers versus words to describe a specific number.

In The Blogsmith Style Guide, writers are directed to spell out numbers nine and under within the body copy, even if they refer to large sums.

For example:

Don't write this:	Write this instead:
"3 million."	*"Three million."*

Numbers 10 and above should use numbers instead of letters.

For example:

Don't write this:	Write this instead:
"Ten million."	*"10 million."*

You'll also want to specify how to handle numbers in headings.

The Blogsmith Style Guide instructs writers to always use numbers instead of letters in headings.

Numeric Sequence Style

Finally, The Blogsmith Style Guide provides guidance to writers sharing numbers in sequences.

For a numeric sequence or range that consists of a number below 10 and a number over 10, use numbers.

For example:

"7–11."

For repetitive numeric sequences or ranges in the same article or in a list, use numbers.

For example:

"1–2 posts,"
"2–3 tweets."

This chapter might feel like getting into the weeds with detail, but when you're creating content on a large scale, you'll appreciate having fewer edits to make to achieve consistency.

 **Chapter 6**

How to Write Engaging and Useful Lists

List formatting is a way to satisfy the needs of the reader while achieving great content success metrics. **Listicles** are articles that follow a list-based structure to present information. Internet users have grown to love listicles thanks to paunchy digital native-focused news outlets like BuzzFeed.

The way listicles present information helps readers quickly find what they need in an easy to comprehend format—all while encouraging users to stick around and read more. Thanks to its increased white space and consistent presentation, list formatting simplifies digging into details. By improving readability, reader engagement (measured by metrics such as time on page) also increases.

For example:

- *"3 Ways to Improve Clarity in Your Writing"*
- *"5 Tips to Write an Excellent Introduction"*
- *"10 Call to Action Examples to Boost Your Conversions"*

List Formatting Basics

To be effective with bullet styling, you need to create some enforceable rules around using them in your style guide.

Here's the most basic rule:

Use bullet points whenever possible to create white space and break up information.

Here's the recommended formula for determining *when* to use list formatting:

If you ask more than **two questions**, discuss more than **two ideas**, or highlight more than **two advantages** of a product in a row, turn those questions, ideas, or advantages into a bullet list.

Don't use bullets for only one or two items—it looks visually unbalanced.

There are also situations where list formatting is necessary when creating content you want to rank in relevant searches—specifically, when optimizing for a list snippet (see <u>Chapter 12</u>).

Since **list formatting** is a special type of formatting, it deserves its own special, dedicated rules.

Here's one:

If a bullet list exceeds five items, consider regrouping information as separate bullet point lists under related categories.

For example:

Don't write this:

"Grocery list:

- *Carrots.*
- *Broccoli.*
- *Apples.*
- *Blueberries.*
- *Zucchini.*
- *Bananas."*

Write this instead:

"Grocery list:

Vegetables:

- *Carrots.*
- *Broccoli.*
- *Zucchini.*

Fruits:

- *Apples.*
- *Blueberries.*
- *Bananas."*

Add a sentence before your bullet list that explains or introduces it. Use a complete blank space (a hard return) above and below this sentence. This separates the explanation from the list items.

More specifically, for sentences with a colon preceding a bullet list, give them their own paragraph (hard return) to create white space.

For example:

"My grocery list:

(this text in parentheses is a representation of the blank space to add)

- *Apples.*
- *Bananas.*
- *Tomatoes."*

Use colons to separate labels from explanations, like when defining a term. Add **bold** formatting to the label/phrase.

For example:

"Marketing definitions:

- **Account-based marketing (ABM)**: A marketing strategy where businesses invest resources on target accounts within a market.
- **Call to action (CTA)**: An element in your website content that prompts users to take specific actions."

You may also want to designate a preference for the visual styling of your bullet points.

Here's how The Blogsmith Style Guide directs writers in this regard: bullet and numbered lists are the only formatting styles used for adding lists to content. We do *not* use dashes or other list formatting unless there's a good reason.

As with other aspects of style, consistency is important when creating bullet lists.

Ensure parallelism between all points in a list. And, in **most** cases, ensure formatting consistency between all bullet lists within a single piece of content.

Ask yourself: Do all bullet lists start in the same way? Specifically, are they all either full sentences or fragments?

If items in a list are complete sentences, punctuate them as such. Otherwise, do *not* use punctuation for bullet lists.[19] That should be the only deviation from parallelism between a document's separate bulleted lists.

How to Write Listicles

Once you get the hang of list styling, including the tips on indentation and parallelism from Chapter 4, it's time to become familiar with a slightly more complex application of these concepts: writing listicles.

A listicle is a type of content that presents a topic as a list. Listicles are notably styled in terms of a repeated format, and writers must have great attention to detail to ensure consistency across all elements.

This is the listicle template The Blogsmith's writers use when creating articles that include or are based around product comparisons.

Here are the various inclusions, in the preferred order:

- Position in the list (even if the number is arbitrary).
- Name of the product.
- Screenshot of the product.
- Tool description/unique selling proposition (USP).
- At-a-glance bullet list of tool features.
- Best [keyword] for: specific use case.

---

[19] This book uses period punctuation at the end of bullet lists to be consistent with Chicago style.

Finally, when talking about pricing, mention or omit the existence of free plans and special annual pricing when applicable. List pricing by month, unless there are only yearly plans.

Here's a basic template for writing about listicle item pricing:

> *"[Free (with limited features).] Premium plans start at $x/month [when billed annually]."*

If there's a specific plan that your target reader would benefit from based on the features you highlighted, mention it in the body copy.

3. Process Street

Process Street is an excellent project management tool that helps you manage recurring workflows for your team. You can use Process Street to:

- Manage company documents such as operations manuals, policies and procedures, and reference guides.
- Create trigger-based workflows.
- Track multiple checklists.

You can even add or invite clients to your workflow to inform them of any project updates.

Pricing: Limited free plan available. Premium plans start at $25/user/month.

Figure 6.1 Example of a listicle item about Process Street, in an article about no-code tools.[20]

---

[20] Maddy Osman, "10 No-Code Tools To Improve Your Freelance Business," *Nexcess* (blog), February 3, 2022, https://www.nexcess.net/blog/no-code-business-apps/.

 **Chapter 7**

Incorporating Quotes and Examples and How to Write Expert Roundup Content

The problem with most low-quality content on the web is the simple fact that it's unoriginal.

Some content "creators" publish articles based on no more effort than a formula that involves:

1. Copying existing text from someone else's published content.
2. Pasting it into a tool that "spins" it to be "different" (by swapping original wording for synonyms).
3. Hitting publish.

For these reasons and more, content that includes truly unique quotes and examples really is a diamond in the rough on the internet.

Style Guidelines for Using Quotes and Examples

When using another person's words or ideas, offer proper attribution to the original source.

If you're using a direct quote, attribute it with a name and link to the source of the quote or the speaker's website. If they don't have a website, a link to a professional public social profile like LinkedIn will do.

For example:

John-Henry Scherck, owner of Growth Plays, sees another potential upside for Google here, too.

The update will "make [Google's] JavaScript rendering tool require less energy," he told MarketerHire. "I think that their rendering queue is very labor-intensive and they want to enforce standards that make it easier for them to crawl the web."

> **"[Google] wants to enforce standards that make it easier to crawl the web."**

Figure 7.1 An example of proper expert quote attribution by The Blogsmith for MarketerHire.[21]

If you're sharing an example, make sure it isn't plagiarized from your source material. Make up a completely new and different example. If you're adding any copy that comes directly from the source material, such as in an outline, change the text color to red to signal it needs edits to reflect your own words.

Use the rule of three when sharing examples to create balance. Humans process information easier if it's presented as a short, memorable pattern. When sharing multiple examples, aim to share three total. More than three examples may be too much to read.

Keep reading to learn:

- **How long it takes to transfer a domain**
- **How to transfer your domain**
- **Why your domain transfer may be taking long**

Figure 7.2 The rule of three in a topic's introduction.

---

[21] Maddy Osman, "An Insider's Guide to the 2021 Google Core Update," *MarketerHire* (blog), February 10, 2022, https://marketerhire.com/blog/google-core-update-may-2021.

Validating Information + Styling Statistics

When incorporating statistics, there are a few style rules to keep in mind to create a great reading experience.

First, when quoting a study, *lead* with the name of the study (with a link using the study or organization's name as the **only** link anchor text[22]), and the year of the study, *then* share the resulting statistic. That helps people understand the credibility of what they're about to read. It also helps them benchmark the information in time to determine if it's still relevant.

For example:

"*A 2019 Chase Bank study found that 26% of students have credit cards.*"

When talking about time, define it. Don't refer to "this year"—what does that mean a year from now? Instead, add the specific year (such as "in 2021"), even if it seems redundant since you are writing in the current year. The reason to do this is for the sake of longevity.

Additionally, from an information integrity standpoint, you should do everything you can to track down the original source. When **citing statistics**, link to the original study—*not* the article where you initially found the information—whenever possible.

Depending on the topic, it may be important to only include relatively current statistics. Don't cite studies from more than three years ago without justification. If you're citing a statistic relevant to the technology industry, the information should be current within one to two years.

Information from several years ago may already be outdated, but its usability depends on the topic and industry. More often than not, you'll have to use your judgment. For example, it's likely fair game to share the results of psychological experiments from decades ago if

---

[22] Anchor text is the visible text representation of a hyperlink that can be clicked.

another recent study hasn't challenged the results in a meaningful way. That's because easily accessible and up-to-date studies are rare in psychology. In that case, you may want to note when there aren't any easily accessed, up-to-date studies.

The Style of Attribution

There are a few style guidelines you'll want to keep in mind to keep attribution consistent across content assets:

First, when **citing another article's title**, it should be in *italics*.

For example:

> "*In her piece* How to Make Money on Fiverr, *Maddy Osman shares her exact strategies for earning $2–3K/month on the platform.*"

If you're **quoting a website**, paraphrase the information. Don't quote direct web copy—it's a duplicate content issue.[23]

If you're **quoting an online review**, cite who you're quoting on a separate line.

For example:

> "I like this product."
> **- Tom M., June 2020**

How to Include Expert Insights in Content

Expert roundups are a popular content format because they involve sharing original content from thought leaders. Some content creators get lazy with formatting and weaving central ideas together, slapping together a copy/pasted list of expert contributions. In contrast, expert roundups are often worth reading because of the useful

---

[23] Duplicate content occurs when highly similar or identical content appears on more than one domain (website) across the internet. It can create indexing confusion for Google robots that may hurt rankings in relevant search.

knowledge that's been curated within the raw content.

But writing a great expert roundup is about much more than the initial effort you put forth to reach experts and ask them questions. To be truly worthwhile, the writer must take a journalistic approach to weave these contributions together in focused, orderly sections that guide the reader through the topic.

One of the most efficient ways to reach relevant experts interested in contributing to online content is to submit a journalist query to Help a Reporter Out (HARO). Three times daily during the workweek, HARO sends out email digests filled with queries across a range of subjects and industries to a large and wide-ranging list of topical experts.

Here are some general guidelines to keep in mind when submitting a query to an outlet like HARO:

- Come up with a **relevant topic**—a question you can pose to experts that's relevant to your brand's audience and would be interesting to read.
- Plan content due dates around the fact that it will take several days to get expert responses. Give the experts you are reaching out to a due date for their responses—HARO will prompt you for a specific deadline.
- Make sure to include all relevant information/files (like contributing experts' headshots) when delivering a final content asset.

Follow this HARO query submission process to submit your queries for consideration on HARO and get expert responses to quote in content:

1. Start with a clear query title that gets to the point. The reader shouldn't have to read the entire query to understand if it is relevant to them.
2. Write a query designed to answer important questions. Your query should pose several specific questions that add value

to your article. What would a reader want to know about the subject—especially if they had a chance to go through a Q&A session with experts? Ask questions on behalf of the reader's best interests. The Blogsmith recommends writers make some questions required and others optional to increase the likelihood of getting good responses.

3. Qualify responses with requirements. If you don't add qualifiers (e.g., must have been in business 10 years, must be earning $10,000 per month, must have a degree in business), then you're going to get many unqualified responses to weed through. Set requirements appropriate for the topic. Once you've set the requirements, HARO will prompt you to share outlet information (where you're publishing the content), your desired HARO query run time, and the specific topic category where you want your query to appear.

View Query

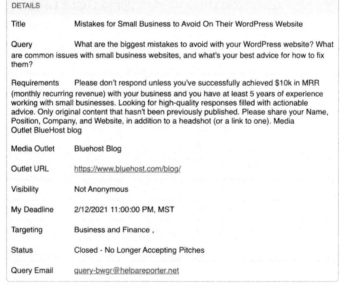

DETAILS	
Title	Mistakes for Small Business to Avoid On Their WordPress Website
Query	What are the biggest mistakes to avoid with your WordPress website? What are common issues with small business websites, and what's your best advice for how to fix them?
Requirements	Please don't respond unless you've successfully achieved $10k in MRR (monthly recurring revenue) with your business and you have at least 5 years of experience working with small businesses. Looking for high-quality responses filled with actionable advice. Only original content that hasn't been previously published. Please share your Name, Position, Company, and Website, in addition to a headshot (or a link to one). Media Outlet BlueHost blog
Media Outlet	Bluehost Blog
Outlet URL	https://www.bluehost.com/blog/
Visibility	Not Anonymous
My Deadline	2/12/2021 11:00:00 PM, MST
Targeting	Business and Finance ,
Status	Closed - No Longer Accepting Pitches
Query Email	query-bwgr@helpareporter.net

Figure 7.3 An example HARO query.

To write great expert roundups, you must:

- Pick the top expert insights to whatever question(s) you asked. Make sure to answer the following questions: Whose answers provide the most value to the reader? Among the respondents, who has the most experience and success in this niche?
- Look for patterns within expert submissions in terms of compelling or recurring topics. These will become the basis for crafting your subheading sections.
- Within the body copy of each subheading, interject experts' quotes with takeaways and other relevant commentary (like statistics) so your copy skews more commentary than quotes.

Still not sure how to put this all together? Databox's blog shares excellent examples of great expert roundup content.

Social media tips & tools to help you be your most authentic brand

Knowing the importance of strategy for creating authenticity for your social media presence, it helps to use social media scheduling tools that can help back you up.

Use a pause button (or create a related protocol)

Says Matthew Coleman, Marketing Director, MyEmployees.com:

"Letting scheduled posts run in the wake of terror news or a global catastrophe can make a brand seem callous and unaffected. By pausing your posts, you can get off of auto and back into manual and be in the trending moment."

Figure 7.4 Example of an expert roundup by The Blogsmith on Fanbooster with special formatting, focused subheading sections, and custom branded expert graphics.[24]

---

[24] Maddy Osman, "What Is Authenticity in Social Media? We Asked the Experts," *Fanbooster* (blog), June 29, 2020, https://fanbooster.com/blog/social-media-authenticity/.

 **Chapter 8**

Guidelines for Using Images in Online Content

Most of this comprehensive guide focuses on writing style. But, when it comes to online content, it would be irresponsible to ignore the importance of accompanying visuals.

Adding visuals to online content isn't always a clear-cut process. There's a lot of ambiguity in terms of best practices. You don't want to suggest an unpolished approach by using visuals that detract from the quality of your written content.

Use the following guidelines to adapt images to your brand's unique style:

General Image Style Guidelines

Regardless of the specific visuals you incorporate, there are some basic rules you should follow to ensure they are consistently presented.

First off, no fuzzy images—you will only be adding value with high-resolution imagery. Just as important is the style guideline that images should be legitimately relevant to the article, not just *vaguely* related to the topic.

For example, if you're writing an article or a section about tips for how to take care of dogs, using the following image won't make sense:

Figure 8.1 A stock photo of a kid and a cat—by Chewy via Unsplash (Unsplash License).[25]

Yes, cats and dogs are both animals—but they're vastly different from one another.

And for Pete's sake (whoever he is. . .), when publishing online content, set a featured image. Without featured images, your articles will look terrible when people attempt to share them, which may deter them from sharing your articles at all.

---

[25] Chewy, Stock Photos, Unsplash, October 4, 2020, https://unsplash.com/photos/ethVHUKAaEl.

Maddy Osman
@MaddyOsman   ...

Hard to beat Anime Lofi tunes while crushing out work (h/t to @flowdotclub):

open.spotify.com
Anime Lofi Playlist (for chill, study, sleep)
Kato · Playlist · 752 songs · 327.1K likes

12:10 PM · Oct 29, 2021 · Twitter Web App

Figure 8.2 Tweet linking to a URL with no set featured image—
it's not very compelling to click on.[26]

Depending on the content management system (CMS) where content is published, you may need to take the additional step of setting Open Graph (OG) tags, so the featured image is properly set up for social sharing.

But a featured image is really just the tip of the iceberg when it comes to incorporating visuals. It's absolutely not enough on its own.

As a rule of thumb, The Blogsmith Style Guide suggests at least **one image per roughly 300 words** (with more encouraged) within the text to illustrate concepts.

That said, there's really no point in including images just for the sake of having them. The Blogsmith Style Guide directs writers to avoid generic stock photos that don't add any value.

---

[26] Maddy Osman (@MaddyOsman), "Hard to Beat Anime Lofi Tunes While Crushing out Work (h/t to @flowdotclub): Https://T.Co/2taALQHOw8," Twitter, October 29, 2021, https://twitter.com/MaddyOsman/status/1454148546345717767.

For example:

Create Once, Sell Forever

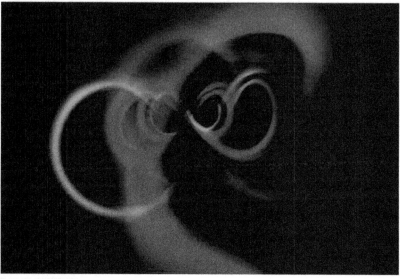

Source - Unsplash

Digital products neither have an expiry date nor undergo wear and tear. Once you create a digital product, you can sell it forever. Digital products might depreciate over time, but you can keep earning a passive income with minor updates.

Low Barrier to Entry

Figure 8.3 A stock image that's too abstract to add value—by Ivan Slade via Unsplash (Unsplash License).[27]

When sourcing images from external sites, you should include source URLs for reference.

---

[27] Ivan Slade, "Rainbow Swirls," Stock Photos, Unsplash, August 1, 2018, https://unsplash.com/photos/mxbhFkoI6AU.

For example:

Don't use this:

3. Planners and Worksheets

People love planners and worksheets they can download and print. You can think of creating planners around any niche, for example:

Figure 8.4 Stock photo without source attributed—
by VadimVasenin via Depositphotos (Standard License).[28]

---

[28] VadimVasenin, "Top View Planners Stationery Cup Coffee Laptop Wooden Table," Stock Photos, Depositphotos, June 5, 2019, https://depositphotos.com/273403734/stock-photo-top-view-planners-stationery-cup.html.

Use this instead:

Benefits of Digital Products

Source - Depositphotos, Standard License

Figure 8.5 Stock photo with source attributed—by VisualGeneration
via Depositphotos (Standard License).[29]

An exception involves taking screenshots—for example, of a brand's website. You can specify this as a *"Screenshot"* with caption text below the image. Format it using sentence case and *italics*.

---

[29] VisualGeneration, "Businesswoman Earning Money from Online Business.," Stock Photos, Depositphotos, April 22, 2017, https://depositphotos.com/150653888/stock-illustration-businesswoman-earning-money-from-online.html.

For example:

Setting Links To Open in a New Tab

Screenshot

Figure 8.6 An annotated screenshot of the WordPress editor.[30]

But just because an image appears on another website does not automatically make it fair game for your use. Refer to Chapter 9 for specific guidelines to determine imagery that is legal to use.

When adding images to your draft, suggest alternative (alt) text incorporating the primary keyword (while also describing the image)—ideally, that could also be used as an image caption.

---

[30] *WordPress Gutenberg Editor*, Browser (Automattic, 2018).

Virtual Card Recurring

Screenshot
Alt: Plate IQ's virtual recurring card for B2B payment automation.

Figure 8.7 Example image with alt text.

Your style guide should also define where you want images to be placed respective of surrounding text elements.

The Blogsmith Style Guide recommends that, when using images within text, they should be inserted after a subheading (not before it). They should also be referenced exactly where they're being discussed—like right before or after the text that refers to them, depending on the context of the text and directional cues in reference to the image.

Search for Elementor and install it. Then click Activate.

Alt: Installing and activating the Elementor plugin in the WordPress dashboard.

Figure 8.8 Example of copy referring to the image below it.[31]

---

[31] Maddy Osman, "How to Use Elementor: Your Full Setup Guide for the WordPress Website Builder," Wp Unboxed (blog), June 7, 2021, https://raidboxes.io/en/blog/wordpress/how-to-use-elementor/.

On a related note, use inline images. Don't align them to the center, right, or left of text unless brand standards specify different formatting.

To ensure consistency, you may want your brand style guide to provide further guidance about specific image dimensions, image treatment (such as adding a solid black outline or shadow), and so on.

The Blogsmith Style Guide also provides basic direction for instances that would benefit from a custom image. For example, when sharing data in table formatting, we send a request to our designer to create a representative graphic. The table tag is deprecated in terms of how it impacts search engine optimization (SEO), meaning you should avoid it. In other words, SEO best practices discourage table formatting via HTML code—they should instead be converted to a graphic representation.

For more regarding writing for robots (SEO considerations), see Part 2 (Chapters 10–15).

Style Rules for Embedding Visuals

As well as adding images, there may be times when you need to embed certain media in content. To keep your draft document clean, it'll help to follow these style rules:

When embedding **YouTube videos**, add the call to action (CTA) "**Embed:**" before the link.

For example:

Embed: *https://youtu.be/dQw4w9WgXcQ*

When embedding long code snippets (like an Instagram post), simply insert the CTA **Embed:** and add the code for the relevant asset as a comment.

For example:

Embed:

Figure 8.9 Example of Instagram embed code referenced in a Google Doc.

Regardless of what you're embedding, refer to it in its own paragraph (not as part of another).

 **Chapter 9**

How to Make Your Content More Visually Engaging

Include visuals with your written copy in an effort to keep readers engaged. Use these guidelines to help select and incorporate different types of legal-to-use imagery.

Defining Legal-to-Use Imagery

You didn't create an existing visual asset—can you still use it within your content?

The answer depends on your response to the following three questions:

1. **Is the asset licensed for your use case?** Many stock assets are licensed under Creative Commons, which sets rules for reuse.[32] While many free stock assets can be reused for any use case without restriction, some Creative Commons licenses require use that's limited to non-commercial purposes. This means that if there's a stock asset you're eyeing for the company blog, double-check that the license specifically covers commercial use.

2. **Do *you* have a license to use the asset?** Many stock assets are available for free, which is why they're often a popular choice when adding visuals to content. Others are available by subscription or paid credits. If you're using a paid stock

---

[32] "About The Licenses," Creative Commons, accessed March 10, 2022, https://creativecommons.org/licenses/.

asset, avoid any potential legal trouble by proving you have a license to use it. Don't lift a stock asset from one site and post it on yours without validating that you can legally use it.

3. **Did you provide attribution?** Some stock assets require attribution in exchange for a license. This is usually a link back to the creator, denoting them as the source of the visual. Regardless of the license's specific terms of use, providing attribution is a good practice for giving content creators their dues. For branded visuals on other blogs, as a best practice, reach out to ask if it's OK for you to re-share. In most cases involving branded assets for situations including expert roundups or survey results, brands want external parties to share such content and will happily accept your request.

The Fallacy of Stock Photos

One of the most popular and obvious choices for incorporating visuals into written content is the use of stock photos. This is because many stock photos are free and easy to come by. But this easy access to stock assets is a double-edged sword because it means your use of stock photos isn't unique or notable.

And if you're using popular stock assets, your target audience may pick up on the fact that you're using stock images and be turned off by it. Seeing the same stock photo used repeatedly by different brands just isn't a great look—it comes across as lazy.

Pe:p Laja ✔ @peeplaja · May 19 ···
One of the most popular women in SaaS

💬 11   ↺ 14   ❤ 112   ⬆

Figure 9.1 ConversionXL founder Peep Laja joking about a highly recognizable stock photo favored by software as a service (SaaS) businesses on May 19, 2021 via Twitter.[33]

However, just because you should generally avoid stock photos doesn't mean you have to create custom graphics for all content pieces.

Here are several diverse ideas for incorporating impactful imagery within your content.

Ideas for Incorporating Legal-to-Use Visuals into Blog Content

Use a Relevant, Fun GIF

In general, web content tends to be less formal than other types of writing. So give yourself permission to have a little fun with it when it comes to adding visuals—assuming they feel on-brand.

Mix up visuals with a fun and relevant GIF[34]—your audience will

---

[33] Pe:p Laja UA (@peeplaja), "One of the Most Popular Women in SaaS Https://T.Co/KgMKQneeUm," Twitter, May 20, 2021, https://twitter.com/peeplaja/status/1395099922052026368.
[34] Graphics interchange format.

appreciate it. Just make sure the visual is appropriate for the topic. A funny GIF is not going to go down well in content that's meant to be serious in nature.

Embed a Relevant YouTube Video

Another great way to mix up visuals? Suggest relevant YouTube URLs to share within content. No, it doesn't have to be a video that *you've* produced. Just don't share something from someone who'd be considered a competitor. By embedding a video, you're increasing the likelihood that someone's going to stay on the page for longer while gaining a more well-rounded perspective of the topic.

You could also consider creating a video version of your article using a content repurposing tool like Lumen5, which uses artificial intelligence to suggest editable captions and imagery.

Add Statistics with Sources

Vary your visuals using a free Statista account. Statista shares data across 170+ industries and 150+ countries, so—more than likely—there's something in its database that will be relevant to your content creation efforts. And there are many other places where you can also seek out engaging data imagery, like Google Journalist Studio.

Publications sharing branded statistics imagery *may* also be fair game for reuse. In most cases, the publications go to the trouble of creating the imagery because they want it to be shared in exchange for a link back to their content. But if you're not sure whether you're legally allowed to use the imagery, contact them to ask and get permission in writing.

Figure 9.2 A visual statistic from NTT.[35]

Speaking of statistics, if you have great data to share but no available imagery, consider commissioning custom graphics to support your content creation efforts. Note that custom graphics can also help make formulas and definitions pop in a way that's begging to be shared.

Here's an example custom graphic that graphic design agency Design Pickle made for a guest post The Blogsmith created for HubSpot:

---

[35] NTT, "2020 Global Customer Experience Benchmarking Report" (NTT, 2020), https://services.global.ntt/en-us/insights/2020-global-cx-benchmarking-report.

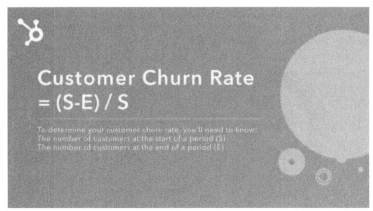

Figure 9.3 A branded graphic The Blogsmith created for HubSpot.[36]

Besides creating graphics for individual statistics, consider going a step further in offering content flush with data and statistics. Creating longer infographics is a great way to increase content engagement, sharing, and potentially backlinks.

Use Examples to Prove a Point

People process information differently. Content creators should use both words and visuals (perhaps even audio) to help people learn things in a way that most resonates with them. Using visual examples for campaigns and case studies can help people better process whatever point you're trying to make.

For example:

Let's say you're writing an article about how to brand your business in automated e-commerce shipping emails. To add depth to your written content, consider sharing some real-life campaign examples with commentary. Taking the time to do this will help people connect the dots between concepts and execution.

Here's an example of a shipping email from Coco & Eve, plus helpful commentary to explain its relevance to the larger topic of

---

[36] Irina Nica, "How to Measure Customer Experience: Key Metrics and Tools," *Acquire* (blog), October 1, 2020, https://acquire.io/blog/measure-customer-experience-metrics-tools/.

e-commerce shipping emails:

Figure 9.4 An example for an article about e-commerce shipping emails.[37]

"Coco & Eve sells hair masks made with coconuts. This branded shipping email is a fun way to spice up an otherwise dull transactional email. The takeaway? There are so many branding opportunities along the customer journey—take advantage of them!"

---

[37] Coco & Eve US to Maddy Osman, "Your Coco & Eve Order Is Confirmed!," Email, January 7, 2020.

Share Use Cases with Screenshots and Annotations

Depending on what you're creating content about, you may want to use visuals to help readers understand relevant use cases. For example, written copy isn't enough on its own to distill complex instructions from developer-speak to a non-technical layperson. Creating content for software as a service (SaaS) companies often involves sharing screenshots and annotations.

Pro tip:

Incorporate screenshots and annotations to help people understand how they might use a tool in their workflow. Help solve users' problems with your explanation of how to use the tool you're writing about.

When it comes to writing content about how to do something that involves a computer interface, grab screenshots for each step. Use software like CloudApp to add annotations that provide emphasis and helpful text, or blur out sensitive information (if necessary). Screenshot annotation tools also enable you to add dimension when creating short videos or GIFs, which can be more effective than a static image for helping readers solve issues.

Figure 9.5 An example of screenshot annotation.[38]

Screenshots of websites mentioned in your copy (or a specific aspect of them) are also a great way to add an easy visual to an article.

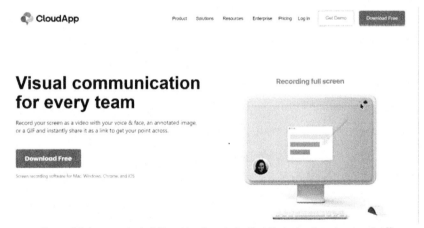

Figure 9.6 A screenshot of CloudApp's website that illustrates the above point.[39]

From a practical standpoint, you need a system in place for your writers to have access to any subscriptions or logins a client would expect you to use to take screenshots. Creating an intranet resource that lists each tool and explains its purpose, plus user login sharing

---

[38] *WordPress Gutenberg Editor.*
[39] "Screen Recording Software for Mac & PC | CloudApp," CloudApp, accessed March 8, 2022, https://www.getcloudapp.com/.

functionality, can help facilitate self-service access to these tools on behalf of the writer.

For example, The Blogsmith maintains several WordPress test environments where writers can pop in and replicate the how-to steps for a tutorial they're creating, while grabbing all necessary screenshots to communicate the process in a helpful way to the reader.

Hire a Graphic Designer for Miscellaneous Design Needs

If you're serious about creating content for your brand or clients, you will come across situations where available imagery just doesn't suffice and custom imagery could have a big impact. You could try to create simple graphics yourself on Canva, but you're probably doing yourself and the content you create a disservice if graphic design isn't your specialty.

Instead, consider hiring a graphic designer for one-off projects or on retainer. The Blogsmith uses two graphic design services—Design Pickle and Easelly—which allow us to maintain a queue of design requests for a reasonable monthly fee.

While advice for working with a graphic designer is beyond the scope of this style guide, here are some general guidelines:

- **Your designer will interpret your requests literally** so make sure you're giving a lot of useful descriptions and not asking them to make too many mental leaps regarding what you really want.
- Don't send an inspiration image without describing how your graphic design team can **make it unique**. Give instruction to the designer based on incorporating different colors, shapes, text, and so on.

- Share the *exact* text you want the designer to incorporate, specifying where and what size. You may want to brush up on some **user experience (UX) basics** if the concept is unfamiliar.
- At minimum, provide a link to the client's site so the designer can determine branding basics. But better yet. . .
- **Provide brand standards** in terms of the brand colors (main, accent), typography (headings, body copy), and logo the designer should use.

On-Brand Expert Quote Images

If you're incorporating expert quotes in your content, consider creating custom graphics featuring expert contributors to accompany your written content. It's such an easy way to add visual interest, with the dual purpose of making the expert more inclined to share the content with their network.

As a general guideline, your expert quote images should include:

- A headshot featuring the expert.
- The expert's name, title, and the organization they represent.
- On-brand styling for the outlet where it's being published.

Create a process around collecting this information from experts during the content creation process, perhaps by creating a Google Form.

Expert Contribution: What is Thought Leadership, Really?

Thanks so much for taking the time to share your expert opinion! Please submit form responses by Friday, 4/1/2022 at 5pm MST for inclusion in an article for   ■.

The name and photo associated with your Google account will be recorded when you upload files and submit this form. Your email is not part of your response.

* Required

What does the term "thought leadership" mean to you? *

Your answer

What does true thought leadership involve? *

Your answer

Name, Position, Company, and Website (ex/ Maddy Osman, Founder at The Blogsmith, www.theblogsmith.com) *

Your answer

Email (to notify you when the article is live) *

Your answer

Headshot

⬆ Add file

Submit   Clear form

Figure 9.7 An example Google Form for expert contributions.

Here's an example of how a blog I contributed to created an interesting visual for my response:

Figure 9.8 Expert contribution image example.[40]

Also consider designating block quotes that can keep readers engaged by incorporating slightly different formatting or designing a custom graphic. The Blogsmith Style Guide designates that the writer should suggest at least one pull quote per 1,000 words.

Pro tip:

Always consider adding comments to call out content features without breaking the flow of the document. For instance, use your word processor's commenting feature to highlight and label text that could serve as an interesting pull quote.

---

[40] "The Future of Social Media Marketing According to | Rankwatch," Rankwatch, accessed March 8, 2022, https://www.rankwatch.com/infographics/social-marketing-detail.

Purchase Subscriptions to Stock Asset Sites

Figure 9.9 A screenshot from one of The Blogsmith's favorite premium stock photo resources, Envato Elements.[41]

While The Blogsmith mostly avoids free stock images, paid stock subscriptions are a slightly different beast. Because not *everyone* can freely use them, you're less likely to see paid stock images reused as much across websites—and content consumers are less likely to be fatigued by them. With so many other options for incorporating visuals, they're probably not the top option, but they act as a nice fallback.

Selecting your ideal stock asset subscription site will come down to budget and industry. Some stock asset sites cater to specific subject matter while others are more general. The Blogsmith has had a lot of success with Envato Elements. Look out for stock asset deals (like Depositphotos) on AppSumo.

Feature a Long-Form Infographic

For numbers or details-heavy content, creating an infographic can help readers digest copy in a different way by accommodating various learning styles more effectively. Adding a well-designed, on-

---

[41] "Download Photos," Envato Elements, accessed March 10, 2022, https://elements.envato.com/photos.

brand infographic can help increase the frequency at which others link back to you. Infographics are certainly more compelling to share than plain text articles on their own.

The infographic can either follow the main points from the article's table of contents or focus on a specific subsection of details. You may want to plan your content structure with a translation to infographics in mind. Alternatively, you can use simpler infographics to summarize specific sections as takeaways or checklists.

In either situation, a little planning and good communication ahead of time will save a lot of effort as you work through a design.

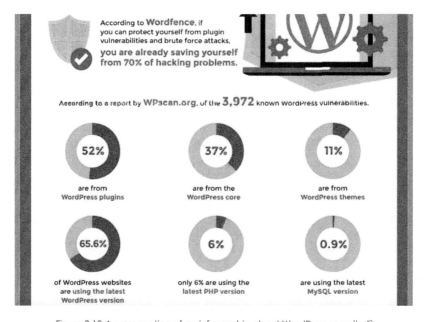

Figure 9.10 A cross-section of an infographic about WordPress security.[42]

---

[42] Maddy Osman, "An 8 Step WordPress Security Checklist for WordPress Security Issues," *The Blogsmith* (blog), November 8, 2018, https://www.theblogsmith.com/wordpress-security-checklist-wordpress-security-issues/.

PART 2

WRITING FOR ROBOTS

 **Chapter 10**

The Buyer's Journey and Search Intent

An effective content strategy involves specifically targeting various **personas**[43] at different stages of readiness to buy.

The **buyer's journey** represents the major steps a prospect takes on the way to becoming a customer. By connecting this concept to a content marketing strategy, you can define buckets of sales funnel stages and map content topics across an audience's buyer's journey. In doing so, you'll help guide users toward the goal they intend to achieve when searching.

The buyer's journey is similar but distinct from the sales funnel.[44] You can think of them as running parallel to each other, with the sales funnel representing a focused subsection of the buyer's journey.[45]

Generally speaking, this includes someone:

- Becoming **aware** of your brand.
- **Considering** your brand and developing an **interest**.
- **Realizing desire** and making the **decision** to convert as a customer of your brand.

---

[43] Personas act as a useful shorthand reference about a specific audience you're targeting. They provide descriptive details about the typical audience member and direction for how to appeal to them.

[44] The main difference between the buyer's journey and the sales funnel is that the buyer's journey describes the full process of making a purchase from the buyer's perspective—oftentimes independent of thoughts about specific brand solutions. In contrast, the sales funnel describes the brand's perspective, jumping in at the part of the process where a specific company's sales and marketing efforts influence the buyer's decision.

[45] "What Is a Sales Funnel? Why It's Important + How to Build Yours," Hotjar, January 25, 2022, https://www.hotjar.com/conversion-rate-optimization/glossary/sales-funnel/.

Explained another way, the buyer's journey can be defined in terms of:

- **Top of the funnel (or TOFU)**: Gaining initial awareness of a problem and solution.
- **Middle of the funnel (or MOFU)**: Anything that happens in the middle of the buyer's journey that involves moving forward with interest, not quite making a decision.
- **Bottom of the funnel (or BOFU)**: Actions that take place right before converting, which typically involve gathering fine details and narrowing a list of options. This stage likely includes consulting some branded sales assets.

As illustrated on the next page, the potential audience for a service or product starts large and gets smaller as prospects learn more about their options—such as competitors.

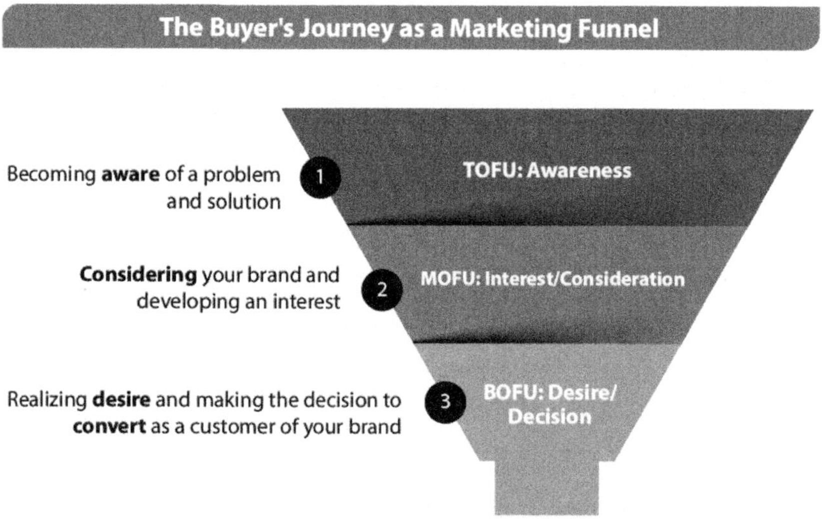

The Buyer's Journey as a Marketing Funnel

Becoming **aware** of a problem and solution **1** — TOFU: Awareness

Considering your brand and developing an interest **2** — MOFU: Interest/Consideration

Realizing **desire** and making the decision to **convert** as a customer of your brand **3** — BOFU: Desire/Decision

Figure 10.1 A visual of the buyer's journey as a funnel.

Now let's look at an example of how a specific persona moves through the sales funnel above. Bob is the founder of BDigital, a fast-growing boutique web design agency.

Bob's Buyer's Journey for Fred's Bookkeeping Services

TOFU: Awareness	MOFU: Consideration	BOFU: Desire/Decision
1. Bob notices that a lack of accurate financials are limiting growth.	4. Bob realizes he lacks enough time & experience to create useful reports.	7. Bob takes a few consultation calls with the best-fit solutions.
2. A entrepreneur friend tells Bob how he keeps his books up to date: using a bookkeeping service.	5. Bob's virtual assistant puts together a list of service options.	8. He reviews each company's proposal by pricing & level of service.
3. Bob tries to solve the problem himself by learning more about financial reports.	6. Bob reads reviews & asks users about their experiences.	9. Bob decides on a local CPA recommended by many, Fred.

Figure 10.2 An example persona, Bob, at different stages in the buyer's journey for Fred's bookkeeping services.

What the Buyer's Journey Means for Content Creation

It's generally considered a best practice to allow for some lead time when you're planning out content creation efforts.

Every brand has different goals, and your strategy will certainly change over time—but the buyer's journey is an important consideration of every goal and strategy. Planning around it ensures that content is meeting your reader and customer at the right stage to make a difference in how they ultimately convert (and with whom).

At the different stages in this customer journey, brands must create specific types of content to cater to the different levels of questions that prospects are pondering. In other words, you must plan content for each stage and **search intent**[46]—across the various personas you're targeting.

---

[46] Search intent is the reasoning behind a person's search query. The specific keyword phrase used can help creators understand what the searcher is hoping to accomplish and where they fall across the different buyer's journey stages.

Tying keyword research to the buyer's journey is a matter of making educated guesses about the search intent behind certain keyword phrases.

For example:

- Keyword phrases such as *"[brand] login"* or *"[brand] contact us"* have **navigational intent**. In general, SEOs don't try to create content for this type of search intent.

- *"How to"* keyword phrases, said to have **informational intent**, are close to the top of the funnel.

- Keyword phrases such as *"[brand] review"* or those that compare brands have **investigational intent** and are more toward the middle of the funnel.

- Keyword phrases such as *"[brand] pricing"* and *"[brand] discount,"* which have **commercial intent**, are at the bottom of the funnel.

Navigational   Informational (TOFU)   Investigational (MOFU)   Commercial/Transactional (BOFU)

Figure 10.3 The different categories of search intent.

Pro tip:

Keyword phrases that include *"free"* or *"download"* generally attract people who will almost certainly never convert to paying customers—so weigh that reality with the allure of high search volume and low keyword difficulty.

Is your existing content struggling to perform? Thinking about the buyer's journey—and any current content gaps—can help shape future content plans.

For example:

- Your sales team is having trouble closing deals, but your content is focused on TOFU. They have no resources to share with clients.

- Your BOFU content is thorough, but you're completely missing content in the TOFU awareness stage.

- There's a mismatch where your keywords are TOFU, but the final written content is supposed to be BOFU. If the foundation of the strategy is flimsy, the potential of the final content piece is limited.

Don't make new content without a plan for what it's supposed to help you achieve.

Defining Topic Clusters

One method for addressing the needs of your target audience across the buyer's journey is by defining topic clusters. **Topic clustering** is a strategy for planning content based on addressing a topic you want to be known as an expert for: in-depth, on all sides, for all related search intents. It involves writing about parent and child topics, then interlinking to all related content on an in-depth pillar page about the topic as a whole.

When planning cohesive topics, execute keyword research tasks around building clusters. Tools like Surfer can help automate some of the topic cluster research process.

Figure 10.4 An example topic cluster for skiing equipment, via Surfer.[47]

[47] Sławek Czajkowski, "Content Planner: The New Approach to Content Strategy," *Surfer* (blog), December 15, 2020, https://surferseo.com/blog/content-planner-release-note/.

 **Chapter 11**

How to Write Compelling SEO Titles and Page Titles

There's a reason why this chapter is one of the longest: the way you promote your content is not insignificant—anything but, in fact.

Sumo analyzed how their visitors read their articles and found that only 20% of their readers reach the conclusion.[48] The majority close the webpage mid-way or after reading the headline.

The famous ad man David Ogilvy has been quoted saying, "It follows that unless your headline sells your product, you have wasted 90 percent of your money. . ."[49]

Think about it this way: if someone isn't struck by your title, they'll never make it far enough to read the awesome content you've created. Your title is like a short advertisement for the full article that will whet their appetite.

You owe it to yourself to do justice to the content you've created (or commissioned) by sharing it with a well-crafted title.

Subheadings also play an important role in creating great content—we'll get to these shortly.

---

[48] Wilson Hung, "Content Marketing Analytics: What We Learned Analyzing 650,000 Hits," Sumo, November 2, 2018, https://sumo.com/stories/how-many-visitors-read-article.
[49] David Ogilvy, *Ogilvy on Advertising*, 1st ed. (Vintage, 1985).

How to Write Compelling Page Titles

First things first:

When talking about titles (also known as *headlines* in this context), there are two different types to consider for web content:

- Page titles.
- Search engine optimization (SEO) titles.

In many cases, you'll need both and they can (arguably should) be different.

Your **page title** does *not* have to include SEO keywords. It helps to have multiple page titles to choose from—expert copywriters come up with several options for any given piece.

> **Pro tip:**
>
> Not sure which heading to choose as your final option? Buffer suggests an A/B test[50] that involves sharing your top title ideas as tweet copy and then using the one that gets the most engagement and click-through.[51]

Headline Formulas

Use tried-and-true headline formulas to write multiple options in no time.

Create a Curiosity Gap

According to Copyhackers, the **curiosity gap** is "the space between what we know and what we want or even need to know."[52] When incorporated in a heading, it's so compelling that a member of your ideal target audience can't help but click through.

---

[50] An A/B test involves isolating and testing individual elements (such as a page title or call to action button copy) to determine which version is most effective at achieving intended results.

[51] Kevan Lee, "How to Perform an A/B Test on Your Website," Buffer, April 10, 2014, https://buffer.com/resources/how-buffer-ab-tests/.

[52] Joanna Wiebe, "Should You Use a Curiosity Gap to Persuade Your Visitors to Click?," Copyhackers, April 15, 2014, https://copyhackers.com/2014/04/curiosity-gap/.

For example:

"The Boston Animal Shelter Volunteers Didn't Expect This Celebrity Guest!"

Copyhackers' Heading Formula

Create a compelling association between your content and something desirable, whether it's someone influential they look up to or something they want to achieve:

[Do Something Desirable] Like [an Expert] Without [Something Expected and Undesirable][53]

For example:

"Make Decisions Like Starbucks CEO Howard Schultz without Wasting Business Funds"

Unbounce SEO Heading Formula

If you're trying to optimize a heading for SEO keywords, Unbounce's formula can simplify the process:

[Adjective] & [Adjective] [What You Are / SEO Keyword Phrase] That Will [Highly Desirable Promise of Results][54]

For example:

"Fast Loading & User-Friendly WordPress Themes That Will Improve Your Rankings"

Koozai Marketing's High-Performing Headline Formula

Koozai Marketing created this formula based on an analysis of high-performing headlines:

---

[53] Joanna Wiebe, "The Ultimate Guide to No-Pain Copywriting (or, Every Copywriting Formula Ever)," Copyhackers, October 28, 2015, https://copyhackers.com/2015/10/copywriting-formula/.
[54] Joanna Wiebe, "5 Landing Page Headline Formulas You Can Test Today," Unbounce, January 14, 2013, https://unbounce.com/landing-pages/5-headline-formulas/.

Numbers + Adjective + Target Keyword + Rationale + Promise[55]

For example:

"15 Free Content Marketing Tactics to Convert Your Audience"

Neil Patel's Heading Formula

Many marketers can't decide whether they love or hate Neil Patel. His tactics sometimes draw ire, but you can't argue with his results. His heading formula is another take on those that have already been mentioned:

Number or Trigger Word + Interesting Adjective + Keyword + Promise (as near to six words as possible)[56]

For example:

"22 Spicy Retorts to Win an Argument"

KISSmetrics' SHINE Heading Formula

D. Bnonn Tennant from KISSmetrics originally shared this five-part heading formula:

- S—Specificity.
- H—Helpfulness.
- I—Immediacy.
- N—Newsworthiness.
- E—Entertainment value.[57]

---

[55] Stacey Cavagnetto, "How to Create a Blog Post That Gets Results," Koozai, October 16, 2020, https://www.koozai.com/blog/content-marketing-seo/anatomy-perfect-blog-post/.
[56] Neil Patel, "Ultimate Headline Formula List" (Neil Patel, 2020), https://neilpatel.com/wp-content/uploads/2020/05/ultimate-headline-formula-list.pdf.
[57] "How to Write Headlines: A Step-by-Step Guide," Neil Patel, August 25, 2021, https://neilpatel.com/blog/the-step-by-step-guide-to-writing-powerful-headlines/.

For example:

"The Latest (immediacy) Research (helpfulness) from the CDC (specificity) about Masks That Work (newsworthiness) (+Tips to Make Your Own) (entertainment value)"

Headline Analyzer Tools

Once you have several options to choose from, use a headline analyzer to create a compelling title and analyze your ideas.

Here are a few great options—all free to use:

- **CoSchedule's Headline Analyzer** is The Blogsmith team's favorite tool because it offers so much value yet is completely free. But it does ask for some personal information to use it.

Figure 11.1 CoSchedule Headline Analyzer result for "Writing for Humans and Robots: The New Rules of Content Style."[58]

---

[58] *Headline Analyzer*, Browser (CoSchedule, 2015), https://coschedule.com/headline-analyzer.

- **Sharethrough's Headline Analyzer** offers similar metrics and actionable advice for improving titles—with no information or email gate.

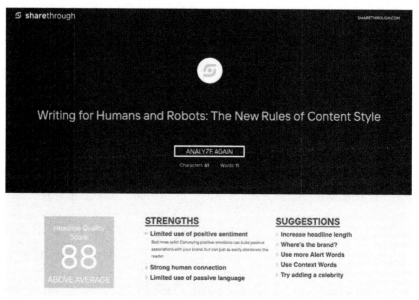

Figure 11.2 Sharethrough Headline Analyzer result for "Writing for Humans and Robots: The New Rules of Content Style."[59]

- The **Advanced Marketing Institute's Emotional Marketing Value Headline Analyzer** takes a slightly different approach, helping you understand how your title comes across from an emotional point of view. It's free but ad-supported.

---

[59] *Sharethrough Headline Analyzer*, Browser (Sharethrough, 2016), https://headlines.sharethrough.com/.

Figure 11.3 Emotional Marketing Value Headline Analyzer result for "*Writing for Humans and Robots: The New Rules of Content Style.*"[60]

How to Write Compelling SEO Titles

It's worth mentioning one more time: your page title can be different from your SEO title (the SEO title is also referred to as a "meta title"). They serve two different purposes.

Your **page title** communicates the value of reading your article to your ideal target audience. Your **SEO title** helps search engine spiders understand the context of the content a visitor would see if they clicked through from the **search engine results page (SERP)**.

---

[60] *Headline Analyzer*, Browser (Advanced Marketing Institute, 2002), https://www.aminstitute.com/headline/.

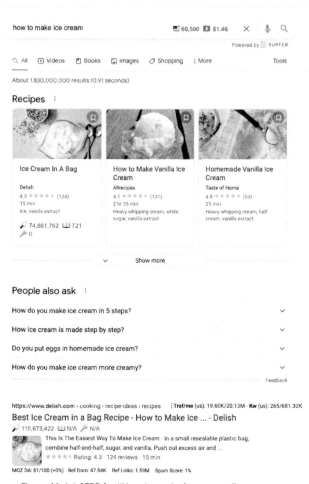

Figure 11.4 A SERP for "*How to make ice cream*."

And while you should write your SEO title with a robot in mind, it must also appeal to the human reader who must be enticed enough to click through. Inevitably, your SEO title will likely be different from your page title. Meta titles require you to follow SEO best practices if you want a chance at ranking in the SERPs. Specifically, current SEO best practices at publication involve including your primary keyword in the SEO title. That said, this may not be the case for long as Google's algorithm becomes increasingly more contextual.

Pro tip:

Use something like **Moz's Title Tag Preview Tool** to preview how your SEO title would look in Google. Limit the SEO title to a character count of between 50 and 60 characters.

Title Tag Preview Tool

Title	Check

example.com > Books > A Tale of Two Springfields
It was the best of times, it was the blurst of times, it was the ...
Display titles in Google results have a 600-pixel width limit, but most are truncated before that at the nearest word break. Moz recommends keeping your titles under 60 characters.

Figure 11.5 Moz's Title Tag Preview Tool.[61]

If the title is just a little short and you're struggling to fill the space, try adding a separator (|) and the brand name.

For example:

"How to Write a Kick-Ass Blog Post | The Blogsmith"

Alternatively, try adding informative brackets at the end of your SEO title that shares, at a glance, what people can expect from the content, such as the following:

- [Infographic], [Video], or [Podcast].
- [xx% Discount Code].
- [Updated for [Month/Year in numbers].
- [Template] or [Checklist].

Ultimately, your meta title needs to be just as compelling to Google as to your human reader. So don't optimize for one at the expense of the other. And don't settle for reusing your page title as a meta title without considering additional optimizations.

---

61 "Title Tag," Moz, accessed March 10, 2022, https://moz.com/learn/seo/title-tag.

You can measure the effectiveness of your meta titles in terms of click-through rate by using a free tool like Google Search Console:

Figure 11.6 Performance on Search results report in Google Search Console.

See Chapter 19 for more guidance on content engagement metrics.

Pro tip:

Here's the SEO title prompt on The Blogsmith's blog post template document that every writer starts a new project using:

Meta (SEO) title: Don't just use the keyword and call it a day. Write a compelling title. Use up your available space without going over—a short SEO title is not compelling.

It's worth noting the devil's advocate opinion that if your meta (SEO) title and page title do not match, readers may not feel their expectations were met. This is because they may be confused if they see a different page title than the SEO title that compelled them to click through. With this in mind, make sure that, even if your page and meta titles are not exactly the same, they should communicate a similar message.

 Chapter 12

Best Practices for Subheadings

Page and search engine optimization (SEO) titles aren't the only descriptive headings to concern yourself with when creating usable content for the web.

Here are a few technical considerations for writing subheadings that both humans and robots will appreciate:

- The title of an article should be formatted as a **Heading 1** (H1). Note that there should only be one H1 heading per page. Each subheading should follow as a **Heading 2** (H2), sub-subheadings as **Heading 3** (H3), and so on (although **Headings 4, 5, and 6** are rarely used). You can use multiple instances of each subheading type per page.

For example:

```
<h1>Title</h1>
    <h2>Subheading</h2>
        <h3>Sub-subheading</h3>
```

- **Use title case for Associated Press (AP) style** but check whether the brand has a different case preference for headings (for example, sentence case). If you're unsure about proper capitalization in either style, use a tool like TitleCapitalizationTool.com.

For example:

Title case:	Sentence case:
"Best Practices for Subheadings"	*"Best practices for subheadings"*

- **Don't hyperlink text or put superscript reference markers in headings**. Find a suitable place to add the link or marker within the body copy.
- **Be consistent by using a parallel heading structure**, such as when creating a listicle.[62] Headings should all follow the same patterns, such as verb tense and formatting.

For example:

H1: *"The 3 Most Feature-Rich Free Contact Form Plugins"*

H2: *"1. HubSpot"*

H2: *"2. Forminator"*

H2: *"3. Ninja Forms"*

- **Keep headings short and limited to one line**. There are three types: question headings (e.g., *Why Is the Sky Blue?*), statement headings (e.g., *The War Ended in 1945*), and topic headings (e.g., *Ninja Forms*).
- **Don't use subheadings for short sections** containing only two or three sentences. Use a bulleted or numbered list instead.
- **Include at least one paragraph of copy between a heading and a subheading**. Use the text to lead into the subheading.

---

[62] Listicles are articles that follow a list-based structure to present information. Check out Chapter 6 for more details. Reference Chapter 4 for additional guidelines for formatting on a more general note.

Here are a few guidelines for word choice within subheadings:

- **Avoid quantifying the contents of the section in a subheading**. Subheadings shouldn't read like the start of an article within an article (e.g., "*X Tips For [the subheading topic]*"). It just sounds weird, and most brands The Blogsmith works with don't like it.
- **Avoid phrasing a heading as a question** unless it's to incorporate a keyword.
- **Front-load information and make it concise**.

For example:

Don't write this:	Write this instead:
"The Benefits of Email Automation"	*"Email Automation: Benefits"*

Subheadings and Keywords

Try to **repeat keywords** in headings wherever possible without being excessive. Use any primary keywords at least once per article in a subheading. Likewise, add secondary keywords to subheadings—but only to the point where they continue to sound natural.

Make sure subheadings can stand alone outside of the context of the body copy that immediately follows.

For example:

If you are writing an article for an HR benefits solutions provider about a specific use case of their tool, the subheading "*Embrace Employee Engagement Technology*" is much more useful and relevant than the subheading "*Embrace Technology.*"

Pro tip:

Separate the conclusion with a subheading following this formula: "**Final Thoughts: [Article Title].**" This is an easy way to use the primary keyword or keyword phrase again in a subheading and signal the final wrap-up.

Writing Descriptive Subheadings

Write subheadings to match users' expectations with the text that follows. Subheadings that are descriptive of the content they contain help Google understand the context of the content. People also scan content with the help of subheadings. Great headings effectively summarize or share the main takeaway of their body copy.

For example:

Consider the difference between this subheading: "Two New Tools"	and this one: "Two New Google Journalist Studio Tools"

The second example clarifies what the reader can expect in the text following the subheading. It introduces a curiosity gap (*What are the two new Google Journalist Studio tools, and what do they do?*). The first example is too vague either to serve a helpful purpose *or* entice the reader to keep reading.

An easy way to add useful descriptions to subheadings is by including primary and secondary keywords. Another way is to relate them to the main topic described by the article's title.

For example:

Article Title:
"How to Rank High in Relevant Organic Search"

Subheadings:
- *"Start with Keyword Research to Create a Strategy."*
- *"Use Keywords to Create High-Quality Content."*
- *"Build Backlinks to Increase Perceived Authority to Google."*
- *"Optimize Your Website to Give Users a Great Experience."*
- *"Track Effectiveness over Time with a Rank Tracking Tool."*

The subheading *"How Google Ads Work"* wouldn't make sense in this example because it refers to related but ultimately very different subjects. Also, it doesn't fit with the title, which promises ideas for ranking in relevant organic search—not paid marketing strategies.

On a related note, **heading puns are fun, but they're not as good as useful descriptions**. If you can effectively implement both, great. If not, aim for understandable over cutesy.

Brainstorming Subheading Ideas That Support Search Engine Optimization

When it comes to SEO content, subheadings play an important role.

When trying to rank for a given keyword, it's a good idea to reference the current search results for that keyword. Google offers suggestions for subheadings (and topics to cover in your content) within the search engine results pages (SERPs) of keywords you're trying to optimize for.

After validating ideas with keyword research, type your primary keyword and see what suggestions come up in the following Google Search feature areas:

Autocomplete

Let's assume your keyword phrase is *"How to write subheadings."* Google **Autocomplete** shares search suggestions from actual user data, including various popular **long-tail** (increasingly more specific) versions of your keyword phrase.

Figure 12.1 Google Autocomplete result for *"How to write subheadings."*

People Also Ask

People Also Ask is similar to Autocomplete. Instead of sharing long-tail versions of your keyword or keyword phrase, it provides questions from searchers that relate to it. These tend to be great subheading *and* featured snippet ideas.

What are featured snippets? We'll get to these shortly.

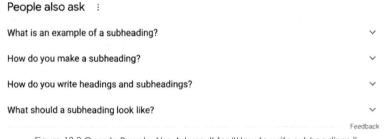

Figure 12.2 Google People Also Ask result for *"How to write subheadings."*

Related Searches

Related searches offer keyword ideas that may not involve exactly the same words as those you typed in but are related to the parent topic. They represent subtopics based on what users are interested in learning in relation to your primary keyword or keyword phrase, and so might be useful to mention in your article.

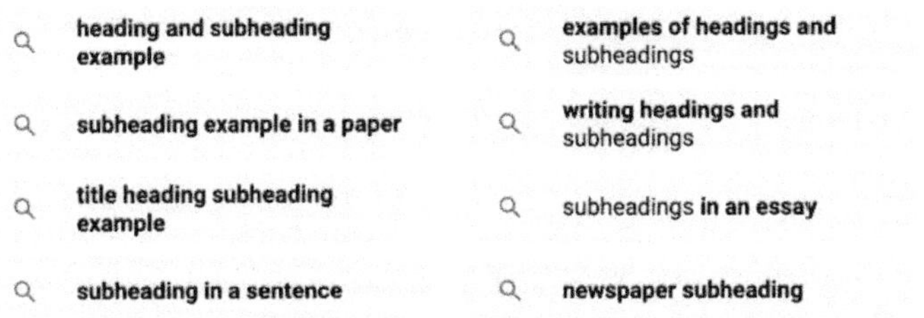

Q heading and subheading example	Q examples of headings and subheadings
Q subheading example in a paper	Q writing headings and subheadings
Q title heading subheading example	Q subheadings in an essay
Q subheading in a sentence	Q newspaper subheading

Figure 12.3 Google's related searches result for *"How to write subheadings."*

Incorporating Autocomplete, People Also Ask, and related search ideas into content (and subheadings specifically) isn't a matter of trying to use as many terms as possible. Instead, pick and choose based on what seems to be the most relevant to your chosen topic and the intended target audience for your content.

Pro tip:

To glean more keyword insights based on Google SERP data, check out the freemium tools **Keywords Everywhere** and **Keyword Surfer**.

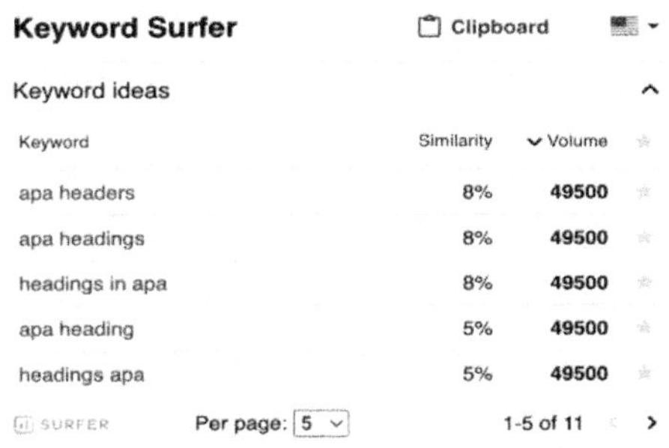

Keyword Surfer   📋 Clipboard

Keyword ideas

Keyword	Similarity	Volume
apa headers	8%	49500
apa headings	8%	49500
headings in apa	8%	49500
apa heading	5%	49500
headings apa	5%	49500

SURFER   Per page: 5 ⌄   1-5 of 11 < >

Figure 12.4 Keyword Surfer results for *"How to write subheadings."*[63]

---

[63] *Keyword Surfer*, Browser (Surfer, 2019), https://surferseo.com/keyword-surfer-extension/.

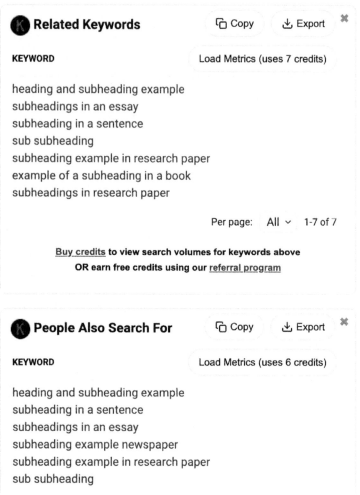

Figure 12.5 Keywords Everywhere results for "*How to write subheadings.*"[64]

Optimizing Content for the Featured Snippet

Optimizing SEO content for the **featured snippet** means using keywords or keyword phrases *exactly* as specified. Featured snippets tend to provide quick answers to searchers' questions, so you'll want to use copy that entices people to click through to learn more.

---

[64] *Keywords Everywhere*, Browser (Axeman Tech Pvt Ltd, 2015),
https://keywordseverywhere.com/.

In simple terms, a **featured snippet** is a SERP feature that offers a "position zero" ranking opportunity. In other words, if you successfully optimize for a keyword that Google includes a featured snippet for, your content will rank at the top of the keyword's SERP.

When incorporating featured snippets, make sure there are no extraneous words in addition to the specified keywords in the subheading.

For example:

If the keyword phrase is *"social media management tools"*:

Don't use this subheading:	Use this one:
"10 Best Social Media Management Tools"	*"Social Media Management Tools"*

Technically, there are *some* exceptions to using only the exact keyword or keyword phrase in a heading you're optimizing for the featured snippet—but don't let exceptions become the rule in your content creation process.

Also, ranking for a featured snippet requires optimizing according to a specific format relative to the snippet type. Paragraph and list snippets are among the more common snippet formats.

For **paragraph snippets**, you want to start by answering the question posed by the keyword or keyword phrase. Start specific, then go more general. Make sure your answer comprehensively addresses the query posed by the featured snippet keyword or keyword phrase. The snippet should be about 300 characters or fewer.

> **Note**:
>
> Don't include any links or images in the section of your copy where you're optimizing for the paragraph snippet. But it's fine to use them before or after.

what is people also ask

Q All   News   Maps   Videos   Images   More   Settings   Tools

About 3,190,000,000 results (0.48 seconds)

The '**People Also Ask**' (PAA) box is a Google SERP feature that answers questions related to the user's search query. Each answer comes from a web page, and Google provides a clickable link to the source below each one. Oct 1, 2020

ahrefs.com › blog › people-also-ask
How to Rank in 'People Also Ask' Boxes and If You Should

About Featured Snippets   Feedback

Figure 12.6 Example of a paragraph snippet for "*What is People Also Ask?*"

A **list snippet** starts with an ordered or unordered list, depending on the nature of the query.

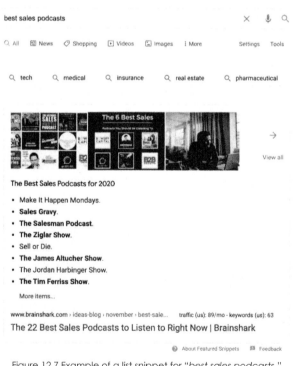

Figure 12.7 Example of a list snippet for "*best sales podcasts.*"

Do yourself a favor and don't waste time trying to optimize for a featured snippet before determining what comes up in the SERP for that term. Armed with these details, create a plan of attack for how you can create a better, more useful content summary.

And don't attempt to optimize for a different type of snippet from the one that's showing up in the relevant search—you don't make the rules: Google does.

To summarize, make sure to check the SERP for your primary keyword(s) before starting new content creation because it's a gold mine for keyword data and structure suggestions.

 Chapter 13

SEO Basics for Online Writing

Optimizing for search engines is part art, part science. There are certain rules you must follow to rank high in relevant searches. That said, the best content is truly unique and written with a human touch.

It's possible to optimize for both humans and robots, meeting the requirements of both. In fact, to be effective, you must be able to satisfy each type of user.

Appealing to both human and robot users involves balancing the various pillars of search engine optimization (SEO).

The Three Pillars of SEO

SEO has multiple pillars. And you must focus on all of them to get results. The Blogsmith Style Guide recognizes three pillars of SEO: **on-page SEO**, **off-page SEO**, and **technical SEO**.

Here's a brief description of each pillar and definitions for common terms you need to know:

1. **Content (on-page SEO)**: This SEO pillar covers how to create and optimize the content on your website. It deals with keyword research and usage on each page and other best practices for Google's indexing of your website.
   - **Primary keyword** (or "target keyword"): The main keyword you're attempting to rank for in search engine result pages (SERPs) with a given piece of web content.

- Technically, you can optimize for more than one keyword, but you have limited space to implement a keyword in crucial areas such as the meta title, meta description, and URL slug. That said, with great content, you can rank high in search for related terms that you haven't fully optimized an article for.

- **Secondary keywords**: Other keywords you're attempting to optimize for. Secondary keywords are often related to the primary keyword in terms of similar words and phrasing and are sometimes also referred to as "semantic" keywords.

- **Exact match keyword**: Keywords you're using to rank in a search made up of the same *exact* keyphrase.

- **Keyword difficulty**: The measure of the level of difficulty to rank in the top search results of a given keyword. As with domain authority (described below), it's measured on a logarithmic scale from 1 to 100. In other words, the closer you move towards 100, the higher the keyword difficulty.

- **Internal links**: Links to similar pages on the brand's website you're creating content for. The purpose for incorporating internal links is to help Google understand the relationships between different content pieces.

- **External links**: Links to resources on other websites. They're necessary for citing sources to any claims made as fact and for giving readers the opportunity to learn more information about a related topic.

2. **Backlinks (off-page SEO)**: Backlinks help you build authority via external links pointing to your website. Backlink building can help you rank higher in relevant search.

   - **Domain authority** (or "domain rating"): The measure of the strength of the backlinks pointing to your website, measured on a logarithmic scale from 1 to 100 (like keyword difficulty). The closer the number is to 100, the better a website's domain authority (and the harder it is to make gains).

3. **Technical SEO**: This SEO pillar deals with the technical setup of your website. This involves your choice of platform, hosting, design, security, integrations, page load, mobile-friendliness, and other user experience factors.

On-Page SEO Content Checklist

Here's the basic on-page SEO checklist The Blogsmith writers use to create every piece of SEO content:

For all content:

- Ensure that the SEO title fits the SERPs (50-60 characters).
- Add a meta description based on the keyword (under 155 characters).[65]
- Write a separate page title option.
- Include an introduction to the topic.
- Write a short conclusion with a call to action at the end based on the brand's goals.
- Add a royalty-free feature image (with a link to the original source, unless it's from the client's website).
- Include supportive images every ~300 words.

---

[65] "Meta Description," Moz, accessed March 17, 2022, https://moz.com/learn/seo/meta-description.

- Suggest alt text for every image, incorporating the primary keyword (while also describing the image) when possible. The featured image's alt text should be the SEO title.

Per 500 words of SEO content: (multiply by 2 for 1000 words, etc.)

- Use target keyword 2x+.
- Include target keyword in the title and 1+ subheading.
- Use the secondary keyword 1+ times.
- Use the secondary keyword in a subheading if possible.
- Add 2+ internal links (*don't* link to the brand's homepage, though).
- Include 2+ external links to high-quality/relevant sources.

As the Google search algorithm improves its natural language processing functionality, the exact number of times you need to use a target or secondary keyword decreases—so adjust as necessary and use your judgment over trying to follow rigid guidelines.

URL Slug Guidelines

Eliminate categories and dates in your URL structure so it's easier to rank for your specific keyword.

Think about it this way:

All things equal, Google prioritizes ranking content from performance-optimized websites. By reducing the amount of text that it uses to make sense of your URL's keyword context, you take a small but important step towards better performance.

Use **only** the primary, exact match keyword(s), separating each word that makes up the keyword phrase with a hyphen.

For example:

Don't write this:
www.theblogsmith.com/07/2016/how-to-get-backlinks

Write this instead:
www.theblogsmith.com/how-to-get-backlinks

Removing the date (07/2016/) from the URL slug streamlines the text Google must parse to understand and index your content.

Meta Description Guidelines

You can find detailed meta title guidelines in Chapter 11.

The **meta description** is the text that displays under the meta title on a SERP (search engine results page). As a best practice, add your primary keyword and a compelling reason for someone to click through.

While some SEO professionals argue that incorporating your primary keyword in the meta description isn't a strict requirement, adding it is a good practice for future-proofing content. Google continues to fine-tune its algorithm for understanding context and related topics.

Figure 13.1 Meta descriptions on search engine result pages.

Subheading SEO Guidelines

Make sure to add your primary keyword to the Heading 1 (H1) tag—or instead to the SEO title if you plan to write a separate page title. As a reminder, there should only be one H1 heading per page. Using these tags helps signify topic relevance to search engines.

Image SEO Guidelines

You can also optimize your images for SEO. Try to incorporate primary keyword(s) into:

- Image title.
- Alt tag.
- File name.

You can optimize every image on the page for SEO. But instead of just dropping in the keyword for alt tag text, try to use it as part of the description for the specific image. Alt tags exist to help people with access issues interpret web content via screen reading software, so these tags should also be optimized for this purpose.

Chapter 14

Dealing with Awkward Keywords and Other FAQs

Google is making leaps and bounds when it comes to its algorithm's understanding of human language. Over time, it will become much less important for content creators to focus on optimizing around exact match keywords.

But thanks to the BERT algorithm update (see Chapter 4 for background information on BERT), Google's algorithm is better at processing and understanding human language, and It continues to improve over time.

At any rate, attempting to optimize for exact match keywords is a pretty safe bet now and in the future. However, even if overt context may never be the *wrong* way to do it, optimizing around exact match keywords is sometimes awkward.

Here are some guidelines to effectively adapt for awkward keyword use:

- It's OK to **ditch articles** (a, the, etc.) within the body copy but try to incorporate them in other key signal areas (title, URL slug, etc.).

For example:

"Building websites" instead of "building a website."

- It's OK to **add simple words** (to, and, etc.) in the middle of awkward keywords without worrying about losing context with Google.

For example:

"Learning to code" instead of "learning code."

- It's OK to **use hyphens** to make a keyword grammatically correct as long as the spacing between words making up the term is the same.

For example:

"Front-end web development" instead of "frontend web development."

Frequently Asked Questions about Proper Keyword Implementation

Here are some of the most common questions asked by The Blogsmith's writers about using keywords—and guidance.

Is there a difference between singular and plural versions of keywords?

It depends on the query. Usually, Google recognizes that they're synonyms more or less, but it also recognizes that maybe there's something *unique* to both of them.[66] So don't ignore the differences between the plural and singular terms on keywords.

When a user searches with the plural version of a phrase, for some searches it means they expect to see a comparison of sites or of products or services. You should also remember that just because these queries seem very similar on some level, it's possible the user

---

[66] Roger Montti, "Why Google Ranks Singular and Plural Keywords Differently," Search Engine Journal, June 30, 2020, https://www.searchenginejournal.com/singular-plural-keywords-google/373297/.

actually treats them as completely different queries and will expect various kinds of results when they see them.

It's always best to let the search engine results pages (SERPs) tell you what the search intent is, so test different keyword variations on Google Search and compare the results of the singular and plural versions.

What types of keywords should I be optimizing content for?

You should use all the major keywords (primary, secondary, and featured snippet). Secondary keywords are usually added to amplify or support a primary keyword, and optimizing for featured snippets impacts the structure of your article.

On the other hand, you don't need to use all semantically related or suggested correlational terms from content optimization tools like Clearscope, Frase, or MarketMuse, but make sure to use any of them whenever it makes sense. These terms help Google understand the overall meaning of the page. Semantic keywords also help flesh out the topic, which impacts the overall quality of the article.

Is there an ideal keyword distribution?

No. There are no foolproof guidelines for how many times a keyword should be implemented. Search engine optimization (SEO) tools and experts usually test keyword density and set different rules based on a couple of factors, such as the number of words in the content and the average keyword distribution of top-ranking pages. The Blogsmith sets a general distribution by word count (see the On-Page SEO Content Checklist in Chapter 13) to prevent keyword stuffing as word count scales up.

Where should you put keywords in an article?

Search engines use web crawlers to understand how pages are constructed—they are called **search engine bots** or **search engine spiders**. They read a page's content through text that wraps around lines of codes of a page.[67]

Imagine the crawlers as readers who are skimming your blog. **H1** (heading one) tags should communicate what your article will be about. The H1 and the introduction normally sit above the fold (before the user scrolls), so make an attempt to use the primary keyword in the H1 tag and in the first 100 words. Just don't force it if it's not going to happen.

Review your H2s (Heading 2), H3s (Heading 3), and so on—do they effectively break down the subtopics within the piece?

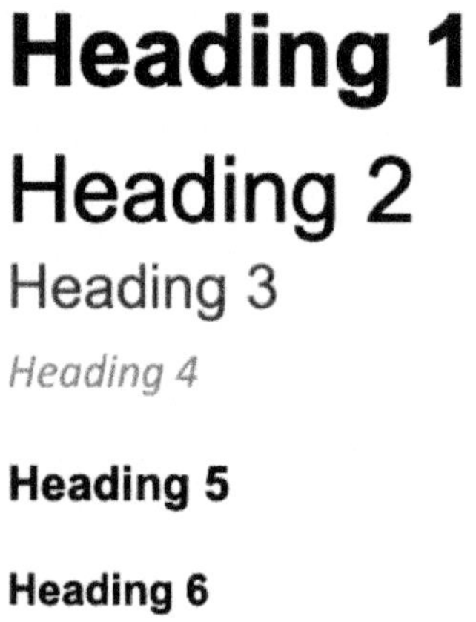

Heading 1

Heading 2

Heading 3

Heading 4

Heading 5

Heading 6

Figure 14.1 A visual representation of Heading 1 through Heading 6 styles.

Try distributing primary keyword(s) within the subtopics as evenly as possible without mentioning the same keyword more than once in a paragraph.

---

[67] "What Is a Search Engine Spider?," BrightEdge, accessed March 9, 2022, https://www.brightedge.com/glossary/search-engine-spiders.

These general rules help search engines understand the content. Don't forget that it's humans who will actually read it. Write your copy accordingly.

If more than one primary keyword is suggested, yes, make an attempt to optimize for each. If there's not enough room for both primaries in the meta title and meta description, optimize for the one with the lowest keyword difficulty and highest search volume.

Can I rearrange a keyword so it makes more grammatical sense?

In The Blogsmith's experience, yes.

For example:

If the keyword is "*what is a staging site,*" you can rearrange it to be "*what a staging site is*" so it can fit more smoothly in the piece.

How do I optimize my article for the right search intent?

To optimize for search intent, it's important to know about the process that keyword researchers have taken: **identifying user intent** and **understanding user expectations**.

1. **Identifying user intent**: This involves examining the types of content and websites that appear in search results for a keyword. Analyze titles in results to determine what kind of content to choose, such as a review, featured snippet definition, long-form guide, or product page.
   The tricky part? Keywords can have multiple interpretations. A keyword like "*cat,*" for example, is not as indicative of what searchers want as "*dry cat food for sensitive stomachs.*"
   With keyword research, we can identify if there's a mix of interpretations (as defined in Google's Search Quality Rater Guidelines):

- **Dominant Interpretation**: What most users mean when they type the query.
- **Common Interpretation**: What many or some users mean when they type a query.
- **Minor Interpretations**: Interpretations that few users have in mind.[68]

2. **Understanding user expectations**: Optimize content by evaluating if your article meets the need from the dominant interpretation or the *strongest* interpretation described.

By creating some rules around keyword use and clarifying fringe use cases, you'll create a more straightforward process to get what you need when working with a team of writers.

---

[68] Google, "Search Quality Rater Guidelines."

 **Chapter 15**

Incorporating Links in Content

Citing sources in search engine optimization (SEO) content is different from creating a Works Cited page, as per the Modern Language Association (MLA) style.

Adding citations online is a little more straightforward when it comes to basic execution: add a link to specific text when referring to someone else's ideas or proving a fact. But there's both an art and a science to the process of incorporating links.

Here are some of the most important considerations:

Link Formatting Style Guide

The following style rules can help you provide the best experience for content consumers interacting with your links.

This is the most important rule:

The text you link to should be descriptive of what you're linking to.

When creating content, you should consider all the possible access issues your content may be unintentionally creating. For example, anchor text that doesn't adequately describe a link makes it hard for people who may be non-sighted or have impaired vision and are using screen readers to navigate the web.

Anchor text is the specific text that you use to describe a hyperlink to content consumers, such that:

Code:	What the reader sees:
<a href="website.com"> Anchor Text</a>	Anchor Text

Don't **ever** link to "click here" anchor text. Instead, use the name of the website or the specific resource you're linking to as the anchor text. There are some exceptions for anchor text wording—find more guidelines throughout this chapter.

For example:

Don't write this:	Write this instead:
"Click here to learn more about Bluehost."	"Bluehost web hosting offers WordPress support."

Avoid linking anchor text that consists of more than five words together (aiming for fewer). Search engines see this as spammy and it also reduces readability.

For example:

Don't write this:	Write this instead:
"2020 Chase survey representing several states and other noteworthy demographics."	"2020 Chase survey representing several states and other noteworthy demographics."

Remove extraneous formatting. In other words, use the most straightforward version of a link.

For example:

Don't write this:	Write this instead:
https://www.google.com/url?q=https://blog.hubspot.com/website/wordpress-vs-html%23:~:text%3DWordPress%252C%2520on%2520the%2520other%2520hand,a%2520single%2520line%2520of%2520code.%26text%3DThey%27re%2520easy%2520to%2520use,have%2520several%2520options%2520for%2520functionality&sa=D&source=docs&ust=1646527008670222&usg=AOvVaw3ZZlvDtfvAo3C1tZxHzTkv	*https://blog.hubspot.com/website/wordpress-vs-html*

Here's another take on this idea using Urchin Tracking Module (UTM)[69] tags:

Don't write this:	Write this instead:
https://www.theblogsmith.com/blogsmith-book/?utm_source=amazon&utm_medium=listing&utm_campaign=launch&utm_id=bookpromo	*https://www.theblogsmith.com/blogsmith-book/*

Don't hyperlink punctuation like quotation marks, commas, periods, and question marks. In general, don't do lazy link formatting that extends past relevant anchor text, **including blank spaces**.

For example:

Figure 15.1 An example of careful formatting with links and punctuation.

---

[69] UTM tags add URL parameters that help marketers track various campaigns and initiatives.

Determining Expert Sources

When including sources from third parties, you don't want to settle for linking your own authority to just anyone. You want to reach out to expert sources. The linked-to websites should be credible sources for any claims you're making.

To determine expert sources, here are two measurable guidelines that can help:

1. High authority websites tend to be measured in terms of domain authority over 30.
2. Hundreds (or thousands) of people and brands link to these sources, including via social media promotions.

Although helpful, these guidelines are far from bulletproof. You'll need to do more to validate credibility, but these aspects can serve as a baseline.

When writing about innovative industries, you must also ensure that sources are timely. For digital marketing, any published data more than two years old is probably already outdated.

However, depending on the topic and industry, there might be exceptions. For more on validating external sources, circle back to Chapter 7.

External Link Best Practices

When linking to external assets, you'll want to follow additional formatting and link usage rules. Here are the specifications made in The Blogsmith Style Guide:

- **Don't link to Wikipedia** or other sites where users can edit published information. Wikipedia images are only OK to use if no others can be found or created.

- **Don't link to Business2Community or other content syndication[70] sites**. Make sure to link to the original article or source.

- **Add external links to define concepts that are obscure** but not relevant enough to expand on in the article. Don't waste word count on definitions that don't add value and won't help you rank higher in relevant searches.

- Use **bold formatting and a separate line of text** for links that might entice interested prospects, clients, or customers to take the next step—for instance, if you are linking to a downloadable white paper, ebook, or webinar. Other links should be referenced in-line as hyperlinked anchor text unless there's a good reason to call them out on a separate line.

For example:

"But now, a new challenge. The key to a _successful client-agency relationship_ is to make sure that both parties are on the same page from the start. To kick this off, the agency must have a **great client onboarding process** to make the transition a smooth one.

Learn how to use LinkedIn to supercharge your B2B lead generation efforts. Reserve your spot for our free, live Mod Masterclass!"

- Finally, when choosing between a direct link to a PDF or the landing page where you can access it (whether gated by payment/email sign up—or not), link to the landing page.

---

[70] Content syndication involves republishing original content to other domains.

Dealing with Competitors

You don't want content creation efforts to benefit competitors accidentally and unintentionally.

Here are a few hard and fast rules to avoid boosting up competitors:

1. **Don't ever link to brand competitors**. If it's unclear whether or not they're a competitor, assume they are. If there's any doubt, ask someone you trust to assess the website you're linking to.

2. **Don't link to *keyword* competitors**. Avoid using link anchor text that competes with the content's target keywords— whether the source is internal or external. Once you've used a primary keyword on one page, make that page better instead of competing with yourself by using the keyword for another page on your website.

For example:

If the target keyword phrase for the article you're writing is *"premium dog food,"* you don't want to use that same anchor text to link to any other page (yours or anyone else's) within that piece of content.

3. **Don't link to articles that are very similar to the one you're writing**. External links should enhance your article, not encourage substitution.

How to Write Descriptive Anchor Text

Link anchor text should be:

- Relevant.
- Descriptive.
- Concise.
- Setting expectations for after click-through.

As a best practice, when linking to internal sources, aim for anchor text that matches the primary keyword for the page you're linking to.

If you're not sure, go with your best guess. One way to guess the primary keyword is to consider the URL slug of the page you're linking to. If it's properly optimized, that's the primary keyword. Use the same strategy when writing anchor text linking to external sources based on your perception of their target keywords. Doing this helps Google determine relevance.

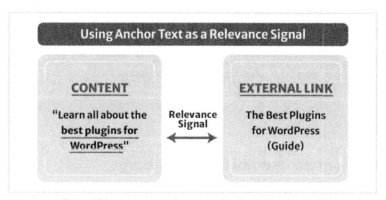

Figure 15.2 An example of using anchor text as a relevance signal for the external link it's pointing to.

Put another way, **use anchor text likely to include keywords for the article you are linking to**.

For example:

If you are linking to an article about the best WordPress plugins for e-commerce, then *"best WordPress plugins for e-commerce"* is most likely the best anchor text for a link in your article.

That said, prioritize natural keyword use over forced exact match keyword use.

You should also avoid **naked link text**.[71]

---

[71] Naked link text occurs when you use the website's URL as the anchor text.

For example:

Don't write this:	Write this instead:
https://www.theblogsmith.com	*The Blogsmith*

Use branded links when referring to studies and statistics.

For example:

"A 2020 Chase survey. . ."

Lastly, anchor text should *always* be underlined to clearly identify it as a link. The reason has to do with access issues around adaptive technologies that may not otherwise recognize the link.

A top priority for all content should involve providing better accessibility for any user.

Implement an Internal Linking Strategy

As a final note for creating more effective SEO content, add comments to suggest links for related articles that you've written but aren't published yet.

Query Loop block. It enables users to display a dynamic

:k configurations and are considered the primary building
it a consistent look and layout across your website.

Blogsmith Team
7:41 PM Today

Link to this article after it's published:

https://docs.google.com/document/d/1vz4c
6rzLkMy96WyY3un6HoPzd_iGazb3qc/edit?u

Reply or add others with @

Figure 15.3 Example of a comment suggesting a link to another unpublished draft.

You may also want to keep a database of content you've published in the past for easy internal linking. Popular on-page SEO tools can also suggest similar content to incorporate as internal links.

PART 3

PUTTING IT ALL TOGETHER

 **Chapter 16**

The Writing Process and How to Self-Edit Your Work Effectively

Creating great content is a *process*. If you don't take the time required to execute each step properly, the quality of your work will suffer for it.

It's not enough to slap together a draft and call it a day. Even if you have access to an editor who can help clean up your rough edges, the draft you submit to them should be free of obvious errors. It should reflect your best efforts to be coherent, spell words correctly, use proper grammar, and achieve agreement (e.g., between nouns and verbs).

You need to start by establishing a multi-step writing process.

The Ideal Writing Process[72]

When creating a new piece of content, do so in four or more distinct steps:

- Writing a content brief.
- Researching/outlining.
- Drafting.
- Self-editing.

---

[72] Technically, there's no such thing as one ideal writing process, but perhaps you can learn from The Blogsmith's.

Figure 16.1 The four stages of content creation.

Ideally, you'll complete these steps over multiple days—this helps you to enter each stage with a fresh perspective that will help push things forward. Leaving time between each stage will also help your brain work unconsciously through any mental blocks.

If you're under time pressure to produce content, breaking up each of the four stages into separate work sessions on the same day can also be effective.

Writing a Content Brief

It's hard to start any content creation project without clear direction and a shared understanding of expectations. Specifically, you'll need to begin by creating a content brief. Much of this involves original manual input. Your brief should address several aspects, including the following:

- The goal behind creating the content, like a specific user problem you're solving.
- The general topic focus of the content, plus the specific and unique angle to take.
- Any project-specific details and features that must be included for the content to meet its goal and adequately cover the given topic.
- For search engine optimization (SEO) content, the specific keywords the writer should include.
- Research material and/or competitor content to improve on.
- The stage in the buyer's journey that you're addressing with the content (possibly communicated in terms of a specific blog category label).

Here's an example of a simple brief for a brand's content project, including some of the above elements:

How To Vet a Content Agency for Your Needs

Business goal for creating this content:	Giving value while selling our services to content marketers.
Target persona(s):	Content marketers within companies who are looking to scale up content creation.
CTA(s) to include:	Link to The Blogsmith's contact page, encouraging relevant readers to get in touch.
Unique angle compared to similar articles:	Strategies and questions to ask a content marketing agency to figure out how to evaluate them and choose the best one.
Voice/tone:	Sort of funny, casual, enthusiastic.
Information the client definitely wants to be included:	Don't overlap any points made in this post: https://www.theblogsmith.com/content-writing-agency/

Figure 16.2 A simple brief for a brand's content project.

Jump to the <u>Appendix</u> for access to The Blogsmith's complete content brief template.

Before starting a new project, you should have an idea of what the content is trying to achieve. You should also have a good understanding of your target audience and how they make buying decisions.

Successful keyword research requires insight into understanding not only the content's subject but also those likely to engage with it. It's worth noting that the reason you want to start with keyword research is—first and foremost—to validate ideas. In addition, your keyword research can and *should* inform the content's structure and how you construct headings. You don't want to wait until the drafting stage to make these determinations.

If this is sounding complicated, here's some good news: when it comes to creating a basic content structure, fleshing out keyword research, and aggregating useful resources for research, much of the briefing process can be automated.

Using Tools to Develop Content Briefs

Artificial intelligence (AI) content optimization tools like Frase and Clearscope help content creators bridge the gap between what humans are looking for and the recommendations made by web crawlers. These tools work by aggregating the top results for a given target keyword or keyword phrase and analyzing the specific *entities* that make up the top-ranking content.

Figure 16.3 Example of Clearscope report for the keyword "*agency vs freelancer*."[73]

According to Google, an entity is "a thing or concept that is singular, unique, well-defined and distinguishable."[74] You can think of entities as related keyword phrases that you'll want to incorporate into content for it to rank high in relevant searches. From there, tools such as Frase and Clearscope use your primary keyword phrase to generate a brief document to inform your content creation efforts.

Some details shared in these reports include:

- Links to top-performing content.
- Ideas for content structure: which keywords should be in the body text versus headings.
- Related keywords to use in addition to your primary keyword phrase.
- Advice for usage frequency (to avoid keyword "stuffing"[75]).

---

[73] *Clearscope*, Browser (Mushi Labs, 2016), https://www.clearscope.io/.

[74] Dvir Keysar and Tomer Shmiel, Question answering using entity references in unstructured data, United States US20160371385A1, filed August 30, 2016, and issued December 22, 2016, https://patents.google.com/patent/US20160371385/en.

[75] Keyword stuffing involves overloading content with target keyword phrases to the supposed benefit of a search engine spider but ultimately to the detriment of the human reader. This practice was popular before Google's algorithm became more sophisticated around context and is now considered outdated and ineffective.

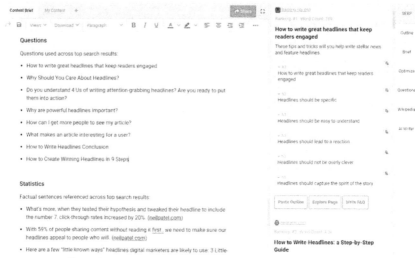

Figure 16.4 Example of a Frase report with content brief details.[76]

A human could certainly execute many of these brief creation steps satisfactorily. But why waste time and effort if you're consistently creating a lot of content and you're unlikely to improve on the results of AI tools? Instead, save your energy for the later content creation stages: outlining and drafting.

Researching/Outlining

Here are three great reasons to spend time on creating an outline before diving into a draft:

1. To save time later in the writing process.
2. To find focus and set intentions.
3. To create a distraction-free drafting experience.

---

[76] *Frase*, Browser (Frase, 2017), https://www.frase.io/.

Three Reasons to Spend Time on an Outline before Drafting

To save time later in the writing process.	To find focus and set intentions.	To create a distraction-free drafting experience.

Figure 16.5 Three reasons to outline before drafting.

Ideally, you'll never go into the drafting process with a completely blank page staring back at you. To tee yourself up for success, designate a separate work session—ideally a day or more—before you plan to draft the content. During this session, you'll focus on creating an **outline** for your draft.

First, collect any information you'll need to complete the outline and, eventually, the draft itself. For example, if a project stakeholder has created a content brief, you'll make the process easier for yourself if you include the important details from it in your outline.

Think of the outline as a high-level road map for what you plan to cover in your draft. Use it to develop the basic structure of your content, using subheadings to represent the major topics to cover and bullet points to add specific details.

During the outline stage, you also need to do most of the research to flesh out the topics you're planning to cover in your content. So, seek out statistics, quotes, and any other supportive material at this stage. Of course, your writing may lead you down a path where extra research is needed—and that's absolutely fine. The outline is by no means a final, polished document—just a starting point.

The goal of the outline is to give you all the information you need for when you start to draft the content. In other words, it's OK to create an outline in a state of research chaos—with multiple tabs open—but the drafting stage should have a singular focus on writing.

The ideal situation is when you've created an outline that you can turn into a draft without further online distraction or research.

Formatting Your Outline

Pro tip:

Need help creating the structure for an outline? Use the outline template that all The Blogsmith writers start with: http://blgsmth.tips/outline

Page Title

FEATURE IMAGE
Image Source

Brief Intro to Topic. Use primary keyword in the first 100 words, ideally. Tease the problem and recommend a solution, then reveal how you'll get to that.

Here's what you'll learn (Add a clickable table of contents, like the one below — making sure to update it every time you edit subheadings):

Page Title
   Subheading 1
   2. Subheading
   Subheading 3, etc.
   Final Thoughts: SEO Title

Subheading 1
Try to use your primary keyword in these subheadings.

2. Subheading
Use your secondary keyword in at least one of these subheadings, if possible. If you're writing a listicle, this is the numeric heading formatting I'm looking for.

Subheading 3, etc.
If subheadings ask a question, start by quickly answering that question in a general sense, then get more specific. This is an effort to optimize for a paragraph snippet, which is usually molded around a question.

Final Thoughts: SEO Title
Summary (not bullet points if you did that in the intro).

Compelling CTA (call to action) — include a link to a relevant page (like contact).

Figure 16.6 Part of The Blogsmith's outline template.

Here's some further outline formatting guidance:

- **Introduction**: Separate this section into the problem, solution, and reveal to hook the reader into wanting to read the rest of the article. The problem statement establishes a connection. The solution shows the reader that the information in the article can solve their problem, and the reveal hints at how the problem can be resolved.

- **Subheadings**: Subheadings flesh out the initial structure of an article, helping to create its basic shape. The bullet points beneath subheadings further define the structure, detailing specific items to be covered in the article draft. Repeat subheadings according to the desired length of your article. As a rule of thumb, aim for roughly one subheading per 300 words of content so sections don't become too dense. A best practice is to offer a table of contents with clickable jump links so users can skip around to the subheadings that interest them most. This creates a more flexible and user-friendly reading experience.

- **Conclusion**: The conclusion essentially mirrors the introduction but without being an exact repetition. It should restate the problem and key points, ending with a call to action (CTA) based on the original goal of the content's creation. This CTA is important because it invites readers to take the next step in the buyer's journey, such as subscribing to updates or making a purchase. You might also take this opportunity to invite the reader to leave a comment with their opinion on the topic or tweet at your brand—this can lead to increased engagement that draws other readers in, ultimately lending more credibility to your piece.

Drafting

At The Blogsmith, an editor looks over and approves a writer's outline before they move on to the drafting stage. This ensures that we're doing our utmost to create content that will truly serve the brand, as well as removing any subtopic ideas that may not add value so the writer doesn't waste time fleshing them out. Having an outline review step also helps to ensure that the writer understands the topic correctly and is not confusing it with something related to the intended purpose but off-topic.

From a writer's perspective, the best way to approach a draft is to knock it out as quickly as possible, without overthinking things. Drafting is about creating a stream of consciousness around the initial outline—but it doesn't have to be perfect: that's the purpose of the editing stage.

When drafting, try to turn your bullet points into sentences and paragraphs rich in detail. Take your placeholder subheading labels and breathe more life into them—adjusting basic descriptions into compelling titles that encourage readers to stay engaged (see Chapter 12 for more subheading guidance).

Keep the goal of this stage in mind—to finish as quickly as possible. Try not to get distracted by further research you may need to conduct or even word choice that's on the tip of your tongue. Put in placeholder brackets (e.g., [more specific word for "angry"]) for elements your draft is currently missing but would take significant time or deep thought to resolve. You can close these gaps during the self-edit stage.

Self-Editing

You may have an editor who will give your content a final review, but that's no excuse to curtail your own self-editing stage. If you've been following this writing process so far, you'll have some things to fix and flesh out that were left unfinished during the drafting stage.

The self-editing stage is where you refine your draft.

This is going to sound a bit overwhelming: *you should read through your document at least five times during the self-editing stage.* But relax in the understanding that you can pay slightly less attention to detail as you progress through each stage because you'll have made all the major edits in the previous read-throughs.

Here are the major self-editing stages to complete before you're really "done" with creating content:

- **First pass**: Flesh out any unfinished sections, refine word choice, and complete necessary research. Make sure that all aspects of the brief have been addressed. If there is anything that you left out or intentionally did not complete, make sure to note it to anyone involved in the process, so they don't try to fill in the blanks themselves.
- **Second pass**: Edit for spelling and grammar. Don't forget to also edit for formatting—this could involve a separate look-through.
- **Third pass**: Read your content *out loud*—you're looking for agreement issues in terms of anything that sounds weird to your ears. It's a lot harder to isolate these issues if you don't physically hear the way your words sound because your own bias will get in the way of editing yourself silently. Another way to minimize your own bias during this stage is to reformat your copy with another font during the editing stage.

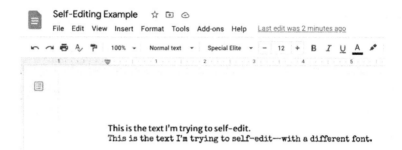

Figure 16.7 Example of reformatting copy during the self-editing stage.

- **Fourth pass**: Validate creating the content by asking yourself, "Is this something I would read/find interesting? If not, what can I change?" and, more importantly, "Is this something that will resonate with the article's target audience?" Refer back to the brief if you need a reminder about the goal and the target audience you've created the content for.
- **Fifth pass**: Check for potential—if unintentional—plagiarism[77] with a tool like Copyscape.

Figure 16.8 The five editing passes all content needs.

---

[77] Plagiarism is misrepresenting someone else's content as your own, either intentionally or unintentionally.

When it comes to creating SEO content, you may also want to designate a **sixth pass** to determine whether the keywords were implemented correctly, the internal and external links were added optimally, and other important on-page SEO tasks.

But note that, although SEO content writing usually involves achieving a specific target word count, you shouldn't create content *just* to hit that target. To a large extent, the specific nature of the topic should dictate the word count.

While actual results may vary, prolific novelist Stephen King has a *10% rule*. Essentially, whatever your final word count, aim to ruthlessly cut 10% of it during the editing stage.[78]

Avoiding Unintentional Plagiarism

Most writers don't have any intention of plagiarizing someone else's work. But it can happen accidentally, and your self-editing stage should always involve a plagiarism check. It's a good investment of your time to seek out any hint of plagiarism before publishing new content and risking backlash that could hurt your professional credibility.

It's OK to use other works as inspiration, but your final piece should look a lot different. Here are a few tips for making sure that you're creating something unique:

- Use completely different sections and takeaways.
- If section headings are similar to source articles, display them in a different order.
- Add new section headings while removing others that closely mirror original source material—this will add a fresh perspective.
- Share fresh examples and insights exclusive to your content.

---

[78] Stephen King, *On Writing: A Memoir of the Craft*, 1st ed. (Scribner, 2000).

The Blogsmith requires writers to include a list of all sources referenced at the top of the final draft document. We also ask them to include sources used to help create content, even if they weren't explicitly linked within the piece. An editor then routinely checks the final draft against all sources to ensure that the content is truly unique.

Once the editor takes over, they run the text through Grammarly or Copyscape to make sure there are no instances where copy is too similar to that of other online articles. They also go through the top three most relevant Google Search results for the primary keyword (or more general article topic) and compare the complete blog draft to competitor articles for possible plagiarism.

How to Create Unique Content

Copycat content refers to similar top-ranking articles that are hard to distinguish from one another. While these articles can serve as great resources for optimizing your content structure, you need to make your articles stand out from these cookie-cutter results.

Here are some ideas for breaking the mold:

- Share a unique point of view.
- Use quotes, for example from:
  - Expert contributions: Pitch experts on Twitter, your own network, or HARO (see Chapter 7 for more guidance around incorporating expert insights). The brand you're writing for may also suggest their own connections.
  - A subject matter expert interview with a member of the brand's team.
- Do a product demo with the brand's team.
- Create an infographic design.
- Commission custom graphics for blog feature images and supportive imagery.
- Share original research or data.

- Write with a digital PR angle.

How to Create Unique Content

Use insightful quotes from:
- Expert contributions
- Subject-matter expert interviews

Get a product
demonstration to better
understand features
& use cases

Create an Infographic

Commission custom,
on-brand feature &
supportive imagery

Share original
research & data

Write with a
digital PR angle

Figure 16.9 Ideas for creating unique content.

 **Chapter 17**

The Importance of Fact-Checking

When it comes to academic writing, research isn't published until it's gone through an extensive peer-review process.

But, with content writing, there are no set standards for fact-checking. It's up to the content creator and editors to do their own due diligence for determining credible sources. And many don't bother—instead settling for one hasty *in-text citation* (linked anchor text to the source material) and calling it a day!

Just because you support a claim with an impressive-sounding source doesn't mean that you've done enough to validate that source on behalf of the audience you're serving. If you present something as fact, your audience will likely accept it as such. The age of #fakenews, assisted by the robust existence of QAnon and similar movements, sets a poor standard for media literacy across a wide population of people.

Do your part to validate any facts you share within the content you create. If you can't prove a claim, it's better to remove it.

Here are some concrete steps you can take to fact-check your content:

How to Fact-Check

Verifying Statistics and Sources

Depending on the nature of the content you're creating, you can add strength to your message with a relevant statistic.

As a general rule, aim to over-attribute: every fact should have a source.

If you need a reminder about effective citation formatting in search engine optimization (SEO) content, jump back to Chapter 15.

Furthermore, don't quote a statistic unless you can prove it with an original source. Verify all claims made—ideally, in more than one trustworthy place. Trace a fact back to the original source and link to it when citing the statistic. If you can't trace a fact back to an original source, either don't use it or mention within your content that the fact is unverified due to the lack of an original source.

What constitutes an original source? It's the organization responsible for first sharing the fact: the organization should be able to back up any claims with documentation such as survey data, experiment results, or other verifiable details.

On a related note, follow your gut. If a stated "fact" doesn't *seem* right, investigate further. If it's a particularly newsworthy topic, check how others are reporting it. It's possible someone misinterpreted the stat in the first place, which then led to others misreporting it—thereby creating a chain of misinformation.

Another consideration for verifying facts is when they were published. Depending on the industry you're writing for, source material a year or older may be considered out of date and of little worth.

You can legitimize the results of a study by sharing specific details such as the number and type of participants.

For example:

"[Company] surveyed [#] people in [occupation] and found [stats]."

But remember: if you can't prove a claim, you should cut it. Challenge your content team to avoid making assumptions instead of taking the time to verify the truth.

As an editor, go back through every source to scan for plagiarism and verify the facts given. Use a tool like Copyscape or Grammarly to catch any blatant plagiarism issues—but don't rely on these tools to catch everything. You'll also want to go carefully through source material to determine whether ideas or content structure (like similar headings) have been taken from work by other content creators without proper attribution.

Refer to <u>Chapter 16</u>, which shares a definition for plagiarism and strategies for effective self-editing to avoid anything that looks remotely like plagiarism.

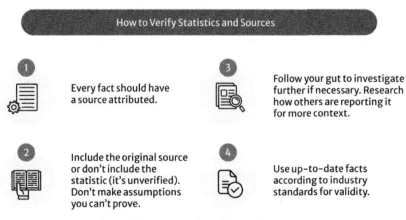

Figure 17.1 How to verify statistics and sources.

Finding the Truth

Just because you've taken the time to include a source doesn't mean it's a *good* source or even that the information it contains is true.

To validate the quality of a source, you should start by determining the authority of the outlet.

One way to begin is to use a domain authority checker. Search engine optimizers use these to measure the power of backlinks pointing to a publication. Although imperfect, the domain authority metric can help you determine whether a site is authoritative based on the other sites willingly linking to them. Domain authority is measured on a logarithmic scale from 1 to 100 and a domain authority over 30 is considered as somewhat trustworthy (use your discretion). Besides using this, you can also determine authority by manually reviewing the specific sites linking to a publication—are *they* authoritative?

However, determining authority is about a lot more than just checking backlinks. You'll also want to determine whether the reporting journalists are themselves credible. Are they prioritizing the truth over their own opinions? And are they expert enough in the subject to justify creating content about it?

E-A-T stands for expertise, authority, and trustworthiness. It's a framework that Google uses to make judgments about authors and publications. The framework exists to help with ranking content in relevant searches, so this consideration is also important from an SEO perspective.

If available, consider checking out reviews about the outlet sharing the content. A large number of good reviews is a great sign—well, unless the good reviews appear to be falsified, potentially due to being incentivized.

In the absence of reviews, you can look for social proof signals like social media followers and a high level of content engagement. But, like most tactics for verifying the truth, this method isn't foolproof on its own.

In general, doing due diligence for validating sources isn't easy, and there isn't a standard checklist you can go through to determine whether or not a source is legitimate. Rather, use the ideas in this chapter to make your best possible judgment. If you tend to use the same sources over time, consider creating a database of trusted or preferred sources to streamline the fact-checking process for writers and editors.

And don't forget to use all the resources you have available. If you have a question on behalf of a brand, get on their live chat or send them emails—as if you were a customer—to get answers to any questions you have about how they'd handle the situation you're writing about.

Figure 17.2 How to determine source authority.

Avoiding Undue Influence

Even when a source may be technically sharing the truth, they could be doing so in a way that reflects their own bias. That may then influence you to cover a topic in a certain way. Others, in turn, may quote your work, so the cycle of spreading a biased perspective may continue.

Clearly, this isn't ideal. Even if your content isn't considered "journalism," you should still seek to share facts with as little bias as possible—or, at a minimum, make it clear to readers what your bias is. That way, they can make up their minds about what they think about what they read in your content.

To avoid undue influence, ask yourself, "Is the title I wrote **clickbait**?"[79] and "Will it influence the way readers interpret the facts?"

Google's Search Quality Raters Guidelines provide an excellent foundation for creating user-friendly content that has the potential to rank high in relevant searches.[80] Within the 2021 document's 172 pages, clickbait titles are specifically referenced on several occasions. Google is absolutely *not* a fan and is not likely to recommend clickbait in a relevant search if there's a better non-clickbait resource.

When evaluating source material, you should use a bias-checking tool to understand the slant that may have influenced the reporting—as well as your own confirmation bias. Nobias is a Google Chrome extension that focuses on determining political bias and the credibility of journalists.

Even if you don't use a specific tool, there's a great analog way to check your bias. Ask yourself whether the article is making you emotional—if so, that may be affecting your judgment of the facts.

---

[79] Clickbait involves enticing readers with sensational titles that don't meet expectations in terms of the actual content.

[80] Google, "Search Quality Rater Guidelines."

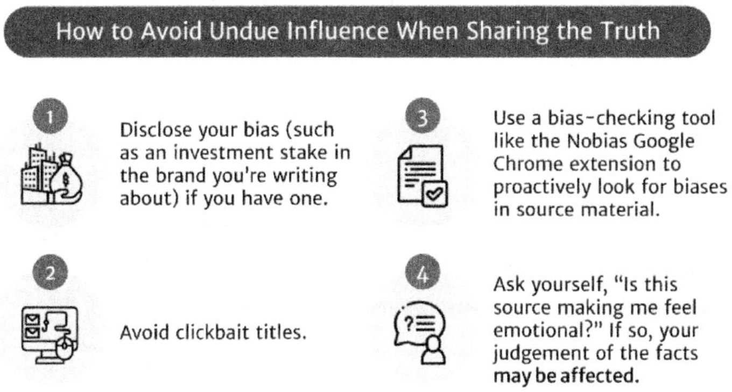

Figure 17.3 How to avoid undue influence when sharing the truth.

Confirming Details

You should also use fact-checking to verify common errors.

Start with statistics and other provable facts. Often, people will misinterpret stats when attempting to rewrite or reposition them, so it's important to verify that they've been referenced correctly.

The next easiest thing to verify is the correct spelling of proper nouns—especially as they relate to mentioned companies and products within your content.

If you want to create goodwill with these mentioned brands, proper capitalization is of utmost importance for showing them you care and are paying attention. You don't want to accidentally offend a client or a brand you've mentioned within your content with sloppy fact-checking of proper spelling, capitalization, spacing—and possibly formatting. Taking care with a brand's preferred spelling and formatting also shows respect.

Pro tip:

Are there certain proper nouns and specific details that continually resurface in your content?

The Blogsmith has basic style guides that the team can quickly reference for common brand stylings in terms of social media platforms and features, WordPress brands and content management system (CMS) features, and SEO/pay-per-click (PPC)-related terms and brands. Your style guide should also include a section for preferred spellings as they relate to commonly referenced terms for the brands and industries you write about.

Finally, verifying facts is about making sure that the details within your content have been accurately recorded in terms of times, dates, locations, and other relevant information.

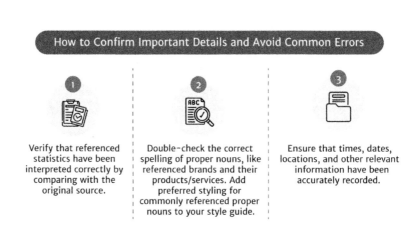

Figure 17.4 How to confirm important details and avoid common errors.

Fact-Checking Resources

When it comes to verifying statistics, in addition to tracking down information from original sources, you may also want to validate stats against credible data resources.

Consider resources such as Statista.com or Data.gov. From there, create a list of credible statistics databases based on the nature of the content you're creating and the industry you're operating in.

Quality Control Checklist

In order to ensure high-quality content, you should do your utmost to have a quality control step in your content creation process. Someone not directly involved in content creation should be appointed to audit each deliverable for factors that include the following:

- **Plagiarism**: Acting as a check on editors to validate sources and Copyscape results.
- **Weird formatting**: Looking for accidental errant characters, inconsistent spacing between sections, and other visual anomalies. The quality control role is the last review a piece of content gets before it's shared with the stakeholder who commissioned it.
- **Client style preferences**: Reading through the brand's style preferences as a reminder and skimming through the piece to make sure there aren't any obvious infringements.
- **All visuals incorporated**: If a visual is still in production when you're sending a draft for review, leave a comment with a description of what will be added and where.
- **All brief elements addressed**: Advocating for the commissioning stakeholder if anything appears to be missing; reading through the brief and skimming through the piece to verify that all requested details have been addressed.

Quality Control Checklist

Plagiarism:
Double-check sources
& Copyscape results.

Weird formatting:
Look for visual anomalies like
accidental errant characters &
inconsistent spacing.

Brand style preferences:
Read through client
guidelines & skim the
article for obvious infractions.

All visuals incorporated:
If an image is in production,
add a placeholder comment with a
description of the asset.

All brief elements addressed:
Read through the brief
& skim the article for
obvious omissions.

Figure 17.5 A quality control checklist for content creation.

 **Chapter 18**

How to Use Storytelling to Craft Engaging Content

Storytelling is an ideal delivery mechanism. It appeals to the child in each of us.

If you've read the rest of these style guidelines, you're already familiar with several elements of storytelling: perspective/point of view, style (voice), tone (word choice/grammar usage), and mood (how the content makes the reader feel).

But there's much more to expand on in terms of storytelling.

It's important to understand that storytelling isn't just for fiction—it can be a compelling part of a business-to-business (B2B) content creation effort.

Think about it this way:

If you can't make a complex business or technology topic relatable to the average reader of your content, you've lost your opportunity to connect with them. Although it may be tempting to show off industry know-how through technical word choice, it can alienate the reader.

To put this in context, recall your experience with business texts and content you've read in the past. You'll likely agree that it's a lot easier to move through copy that offers anecdotes and examples rather than read text that may appear devoid of meaningful application.

Telling stories in your content is a great way to break down complex topics, improve understanding, and retain your audience's attention.

The Elements of a Story

Several elements make up a story, and each one deserves your attention.

Here's a simple non-fiction story for the fictional Fred's Digital Agency CPA (Certified Public Accountant) service:

> *Bob is the founder of BDigital, a boutique web design agency. He is growing his customer base and the team rapidly—an awesome employer and vendor to those he works with. He's great at sales but not-so-great at administrative tasks like bookkeeping. He's starting to fall behind with monthly financial reporting, and it's creating limitations for expansion since he doesn't have enough accurate data to make decisions with.*

> *Bob realizes he needs to hire some specialized help. He starts by trying an online bookkeeping service for the masses, called Accounting 4 All. After just a few months of working with them, he realizes that it's not a fit. He's getting burned by partnering with a team that never took the time to understand his business. He looks around and finds an amazing local CPA, Fred, with tons of experience in his industry. Once they start working together, Bob never looks back. Working with a great accountant like Fred empowers Bob to employ more people and help more clients achieve their goals. Go Bob!*

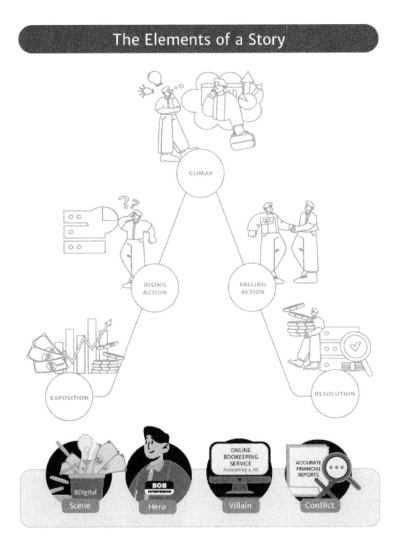

Figure 18.1 The elements of a story, from start to finish.

Here's some guidance for developing each story element:

Creating Characters

For B2B businesses, characters can take on several different forms. They can be real or fictional people, helping to illustrate relatable examples for your audience. They can also be abstract concepts, if necessary.

Start by defining a hero and a villain. Often, brands position the customer as the hero and the problem they're trying to solve (which the brand can help with) as the villain.

Your hero customer characters can also serve as personas to consult when making decisions on behalf of your audience.

In the example story, Bob is the hero, the online bookkeeping service is one of the "villains," and Fred is a supportive character in Bob's journey.

Setting the Scene

An essential part of any story is clarifying details of the setting or context. These storytelling elements include basics such as the physical location and time of day—essentially, the *when* and the *where*. As in real life, a change in setting can open up possibilities and give people a new perspective.

In terms of B2B content, setting the scene might involve discussing the specific circumstances in which the brand can best help the story's hero. For example, if you're an accounting firm, you may determine that your hero target customer has a year-round need for bookkeeping help, or perhaps they just need help with tax prep at the end of the fiscal year.

Nevertheless, you can always tell different stories (although perhaps not in the same piece of content) for multiple hero personas.

In the example story, the scene is the work environment Bob has created and a snapshot of where he's at in his business.

Fleshing Out a Story with Details

One of the reasons storytelling works is because adding detail adds dimension. Consider how much easier it is to remember concepts when given extra details as examples or reminders. The goal is for readers to visualize what you're describing and remember it.

In the example story, details like giving each character a name help the reader keep track of what's going on.

Conflict

The best place to introduce a conflict in online content is at the very beginning of the piece—the introduction (see Appendix for our outline template, which sets you up to share a problem and solution). This is your opportunity to find a way to engage the reader by addressing the problems that brought them to you and keeping them on board until you find a resolution.

How you describe the conflict should compel the reader to act urgently to find a solution.

In the example story, the conflict is the lack of reliable financial data that gets in the way of further growth.

The Plot

When it comes to storytelling in corporate content creation, creating a tangible plot may not be as hard as it is in fiction. That said, you still need to have a reason for creating content. Even if you don't have a "plot" per se, make sure you have a purpose for every included aspect.

Exposition/Introduction

The introduction is ideal for introducing the main character (hero) and the conflict (villain), thereby setting the scene.

In the example story, the introduction sets the scene for why Bob would benefit from hiring a specialist bookkeeper/accountant.

Rising/Falling Actions

Instead of the quasi-bell curve representing the rise and fall of action throughout a fictional story, you can think of storytelling in B2B content consisting of several continuous bell curves. Each section (subheading) represents a self-contained "story" of sorts.

Here's how rising and falling action plays out in the story:

- Bob realizes he needs to hire specialized help and evaluates a bookkeeping service for the masses (rising action).
- Bob manages to grow with the help of Fred (falling action).

Climax

The climax happens every time you help readers come to a realization that they didn't have before reading your content. It occurs whenever a light bulb goes on in a reader's head, and it can happen multiple times throughout a content piece.

In the example story, the climax occurs when Bob realizes that a specialized accountant is the best-fit solution to his financial reporting problems—and makes better decisions to grow the business.

Resolution

The resolution is revealed throughout the content, supported by each section. Each section strengthens your content's ability to solve the reader's problem. In the conclusion, you reflect on all the ways you've resolved the conflict throughout the content.

Make sure to answer questions such as, "What have you suggested that can make the reader's life better?" and, "What was the proposed outcome to the problem identified at the beginning of the article?"

In the example story, it all comes together when Bob finds his best fit accounting solution—an individual with industry experience, Fred.

 **Chapter 19**

How to Validate Content Effectiveness: A Beginner's Guide

Creating content for content's sake isn't much of a goal. Instead, you want to create specific, measurable, attainable, relevant, and time-bound (SMART) goals to effectively measure the impact of your content investment.[81]

Here's an example of a SMART content goal that could guide your team's efforts:

Goal: An eyeglass brand wants to write and publish an in-depth guide for how to pick blue light blocking glasses in October to promote holiday gift purchases.

- **S**: *Specifically*, they may want this content to generate five new customers each month leading to Black Friday.
- **M**: They use Google Analytics goals they've set up to *measure* progress towards generating five new customers each month (and other goals).
- **A**: They've determined that this goal is *attainable* by analyzing past content performance (Google Analytics data) and by creating new content based on published content that's led to an average of five new customers per month.
- **R**: This content is *relevant* because they're creating it for an audience that is evaluating options, including the brand's offering.

---

[81] George T Doran, "There's a S.M.A.R.T. Way to Write Management's Goals and Objectives," *Management Review* 70, no. 11 (1981): 35–36.

- **T**: The goal around this content creation effort is *time-bound* because there's a stated plan and reason for when the guide must be completed and published.

There are many different ways you could determine how effectively your content is meeting stated goals. There are tools to analyze and measure progress by defining specific key performance indicators (KPIs) to judge effectiveness.

Goals and Calls to Actions

What do you want your audience to do when engaging with your brand on its website or social channels?

Answering this question about your marketing goals will help to determine the call to action (CTA) text you use in copy.

Regardless of the medium, **a CTA is important because it invites readers to take the next step**: to subscribe, make a purchase, and so on.

You might also take this opportunity to invite the reader to leave a comment with their opinion on the topic, or tweet at your brand—this can help increase engagement and draw other readers in.

Note: In general, **social media is not a great place to directly make sales**, so think more "top of the funnel" (refer back to Chapter 10 for more about the buyer's journey) in terms of the goals and copy you're using to get people to engage with your brand. Depending on the search intent behind a specific blog topic, you can be more direct. If your CTA is not effective, consider the following:

Reasons Why a CTA Isn't Working to Accomplish Goals

- Your CTA/offer isn't clear.
- Your CTA/offer isn't compelling.
- Your content/offer isn't what your potential clients expected.
- You included too many competing CTAs (each post should focus on one only).

Language Guidelines for CTAs

- A CTA shouldn't be wishy-washy. Be direct—ask for what you want.

For example:

Don't write this:	Write this instead:
"Feel free to get in touch."	*"Get in touch."*

- Use strong action verbs to communicate confidence and motivate readers to respond.[82]
- Use "you" language—speak directly to the reader and reflect what they want in the language you use to get them to act.
- Decide whether you want to motivate with positivity...

For example:

"Do this and your life will improve."

...or negativity...

For example:

"Don't do this and your life will get worse!"

---

[82] The Weinstein Organization (not to be confused with disgraced film producer Harvey Weinstein) offers a useful power words reference:
https://www.twochicago.com/blog/index.php/2017/10/03/37-power-words-use-direct-response-marketing/

- Be specific regarding what the person will get by responding to the CTA.

For example:

"Sign up for a 14-day free trial of our complete software suite."

Common CTAs

- Sign up for a free trial.
- Try for free.
- Get started.
- Learn more about [topic].
- Schedule a demo.
- Get in touch.
- Sign up for a Premium plan.
- Buy [product] now.
- Try [service] today.
- Start an order.
- Shop now.
- Tweet your thoughts at @[brand].
- Leave a comment.
- Test out [feature] for yourself: [link].

Tools for Measuring Content Goals and Effectiveness

"Half the money I spend on advertising is wasted; the trouble is I don't know which half."[83]

This quote has been attributed to multiple different people, but regardless of its original source, the sentiment rings true as a sore spot for many traditional marketers. The great thing about online content creation is that you have access to so many (often free) tools

---

[83] George Bradt, "Wanamaker Was Wrong -- The Vast Majority Of Advertising Is Wasted," Forbes, September 14, 2016, https://www.forbes.com/sites/georgebradt/2016/09/14/wanamaker-was-wrong-the-vast-majority-of-advertising-is-wasted/.

that you should never have to wonder about the effectiveness of your efforts.

The key to success is, well, carefully defining what that means for you. Ask yourself, "What needs to happen for an investment in content to pay for itself?" Then, work backward to define KPIs and methods for tracking them.

It's worth emphasizing that just because you put measurement tools in place, it doesn't mean they're actually useful until you take the time to review and make sense of the data they produce.

Here are a few useful content analysis functions and suggested tools for measuring success:

Website Analytics: Google Analytics

Having a website analytics tool is really the bare minimum for judging content effectiveness. If your brand has a website intended for the public, install a website analytics tool as soon as it launches.

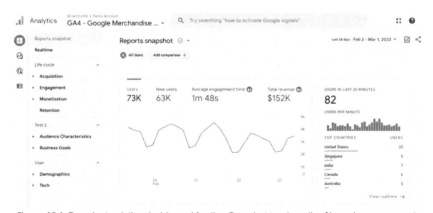

Figure 19.1 Google Analytics dashboard for the Google Merchandise Store demo account.

Even if you don't plan to interpret the data right away, you still want to be gathering data to act as a benchmark over time. This data can help you see how effective you were at the start and how improvements in your content strategy become more effective over time.

Google Analytics is one of the best tools for this purpose. For most use cases, even fairly advanced customization (such as with reports and goal tracking), the platform is completely free to use.

There are multiple ways to break down and analyze data within Google Analytics. Some of the most popular reports cover audience, acquisition, and behavior. You can also set up specific goals to measure whatever you consider to be a conversion (or even a micro-conversion).

If you're concerned about privacy (or do business with the European Union and are worried about GDPR), one of the most popular Google Analytics alternatives is Fathom Analytics. It's not free, but it prioritizes obscuring personally identifiable data related to your website visitors without compromising your access to useful data insights.

Heatmap: Hotjar

Heatmaps provide a useful visual tool for helping content creators understand how their audience is interacting with their content. Specifically, they can help you see exactly where on a page people are looking and clicking, based on mouse movements.

Use this information to understand which aspects of your content people enjoy—and where they lose interest. Some heatmap tools also offer video user session recordings, so you can visualize a larger sequence of events as individual users interact with your website.

Hotjar is a popular solution for heatmaps and recordings. Pricing is affordable, with a functional free plan available for those with a couple of thousand pageviews per day or fewer. Microsoft Clarity is an up-and-coming alternative that's completely free to use.

Keyword Rank Tracking: Ahrefs

Not all web content is created to rank in relevant search, but it's certainly a major reason for creating it. If publishing search engine optimization (SEO) content is part of your brand marketing strategy, you'll want to use a tracking tool to measure your keyword rankings.

With so many options at multiple different price points, it's hard for a beginner to evaluate their perfect fit. Budget should definitely be factored in, but the best all-in-one SEO tools start at around $99/month.[84] If you only need rank tracking functionality or can live with less exact data, you can get by with a much-reduced budget.

Ahrefs is an all-in-one SEO tool that can be used for keyword research, backlink monitoring, technical website audits, and rank tracking. It's a great option if you're performing a range of SEO tasks for your brand or clients. As with most rank-tracking tools, you can set it up to track the keywords your website is currently ranking in relevant search, with alerts for when these rankings change (which may be a sign that you need to update your content).

A scalable option that focuses primarily on keyword rank tracking is SerpWatch.

Engagement Key Performance Indicators

Some of this chapter originally appeared as an article I wrote for *Search Engine Journal*.[85]

In some cases, the specific tools you use to measure content effectiveness will dictate the metrics you can measure. That said, not every metric will be relevant to your specific content strategy.

---

[84] "Moz Pro Pricing," Moz, accessed March 11, 2022, https://moz.com/products/pro/pricing; "Plans & Pricing," Ahrefs, accessed March 11, 2022, https://ahrefs.com/pricing.

[85] Maddy Osman, "Top 10 User Engagement KPIs to Measure," Search Engine Journal, February 3, 2019, https://www.searchenginejournal.com/content-marketing-kpis/user-engagement-metrics/.

As a result, you'll want to define the KPIs that matter most for *your* content creation efforts.

Here's what you need to know about the most common content KPIs—most of which can be tracked in Google Analytics:

Conversion Rate

Conversion rate is arguably the most important content engagement metric—but it means different things to different content teams.

The **conversion rate** is the percentage of website visitors who complete desired actions. A high conversion rate tells you that your marketing tactics are effective because they have resulted in your website visitors completing your end goal.

If you're selling something, the most important conversion rate to measure is when content leads to a sale. That said, your content strategy may not be focused on sales. Instead, it may act as a top-of-the-funnel acquisition strategy that *eventually* leads to a sale but isn't directly attributable to one.

As such, in addition to measuring a conversion rate that involves sales, you may also want to measure micro-conversions. These involve the specific actions you've determined that prospects make on the way to a sale.

Some micro-conversion examples include:

- Booking a meeting.
- Watching a demo of your product.
- Signing up for an email newsletter.

Pageviews

Pageviews, sessions, and users are the most common metrics used to indicate traffic on your website. **Pageviews** are the most "basic" of all user engagement metrics, measuring a "hit" or an instance of a user visiting a particular page on your website.

Measuring pageviews can help you understand how often people visit your website. A higher number of pageviews can be assumed to be an indicator of interest and good SEO practices, since search engines can be major drivers of traffic to websites.

Conversely, pageviews can also indicate that people are poking around your website because they can't find what they're looking for. Pageviews show traffic—but without tying in the context of other related metrics, you won't fully understand the meaning behind these numbers.

Time on Page

So many websites churn out bland copycat content on a regular basis. To rise above mediocrity, it's important to measure and react to how much time people actually spend on your content.

There are two ways to look at time spent:

1. **Micro view**: Time spent on page.
2. **Macro view**: The *average* session duration or *average* time spent on site.

Time Spent on Page

This is fairly straightforward: **time spent on page** measures the time a user spends *on a page* on your website.

This metric provides an indication of interest.

Average Session Duration

Average session duration measures the length of an average session (**session duration**) over a specific time period, divided by the total **number of sessions** during that time.

Session refers to a group of user interactions with your website. The average session duration refers to the average total time spent on your website. This is different from **time spent on page** because it tracks *all* the activity a visitor has completed on your website versus tracking only the time spent on a certain page.

Bounce Rate

Closely related to time spent on page is the bounce rate. A common trend observed is that the bounce rate is inversely proportional to the average session duration. In other words, as the bounce rate increases, the average session duration decreases.

The **bounce rate** is the percentage of website visitors who exit after only viewing one page. The bounce rate gives an indication of how good your content is because if people are leaving without taking action, then your content isn't doing its job.

People may bounce for several reasons:

- Your CTA/offer isn't clear.
- Your content/offer isn't what they expected.
- They got bored.
- You're not offering anything different.

While it is important to measure how engaged your visitors are, it's also important to measure how *unengaged* they are. You might have high traffic numbers, but if you also have high bounce rates, this means your content isn't engaging enough to make website visitors stick around.

Top Exit Pages

Exit pages are the last pages accessed before leaving a website. The **exit rate** measures the percentage of people who leave your website from the exit page.

The exit pages (and, subsequently, the exit rates) are related to bounce rates in that they both consider the last pages a visitor goes to on a website. The main difference between these metrics is that the bounce rate takes into consideration the number of visitors who exit your website after visiting *a single page*.

Calculating the exit rate can be helpful, especially when your website encourages customers to follow a certain path (the buyer's journey—see Chapter 10). Knowing your top exit pages can help you make sense of *why* your exit rate is the way it is.

Some pages are designed to have high exit rates, such as your contact page or a "thank you" page.[86] When a page is designated as an exit page, a high exit rate indicates that customers completed the desired action.

A high exit rate on a non-exit page can be caused by:

- Poorly organized information on your website (hierarchical issues).
- A missing CTA (so the person exits the website without further action).
- An overwhelming amount of information.
- Lacking or missing information.

Pages per Session

Another way of measuring interest in your content is **pages per session**, or the number of unique page visits per session.

From a business perspective, the higher the pages per session metric, the better. This is because a high pages per session count shows that your website visitors looked around and visited more than one page—thereby truly engaging with your website.

Bounce rates are similar to pages per session, but while bounce rates look at the *next* step (or page), pages per session looks at the *whole path* the visitor follows.

---

[86] A "thank you" page is where visitors are redirected after completing a conversion action. A tracking code can be placed on a "thank you" page for easy measurement of goal completion.

Page/Scroll Depth

Page (or scroll) depth measures how thoroughly your audience is consuming your content by tracking where on the page people stop reading.

This can indicate two things:

1. **Readability**: If your content is easy to read, people will go further down the page.
2. **Interest**: Assume that the further people scroll down your page, the more they want to consume your content.

Unique Visitors

Unique visitor is a term used to refer to a person who visits a website at least once during the reporting period. Google Analytics puts more emphasis on tracking page views (or visits) but the unique visitors metric shows how many *individuals* your website reaches.

New Visitors versus Returning Visitors

New users are people accessing your website for the first time *on a specific device.*

Google uses client IDs to track users. If you're using a mobile phone to access a website, *then* using your desktop to visit the same website again (the first time on a desktop), Google counts this activity as two new visitors (unless you're signed into the same Google Chrome account on both devices).

Returning visitors are those who have previously visited your website. Specifically, Google Analytics 4 defines new users within a 26-month time frame (website owners can set a shorter time frame).[87] If you revisit a website within the two-year time frame, you are considered a returning visitor, but if you revisit the website after

---

[87] "Data Retention - Analytics Help," Google, accessed March 9, 2022, https://support.google.com/analytics/answer/7667196?hl=en.

more than two years, you'll be counted as a new visitor again.

This metric is presented as a pie graph, comparing the ratio between the two dimensions: new and returning visitors.

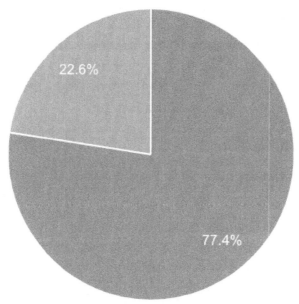

Figure 19.1 New visitors compared to returning visitors in a pie graph on the Universal Analytics report.

Impressions

Impressions measure the number of times your content is seen by a consumer in a given situation. As they relate to search, impressions measure how many times your content is seen in a search for a specific keyword over a specific time period (such as a month).

Impressions are basic measurements that don't provide a lot of context but—in general—the higher your impressions, the better. It's a good metric for judging overall success with a content promotion strategy, month after month. Measuring impressions can also be helpful in identifying and understanding trends.

Click-Through Rate

The click-through rate (CTR) measures the number of people who clicked a link compared to the total impressions for that link. As it relates to search, CTR measures the proportion of users who click on your content over the total number of those who saw it on the search engine results pages (SERPs). Put more simply, CTR equals clicks divided by impressions.

A low CTR may indicate that your meta title or meta description isn't very compelling. Alternatively, it may indicate that the way you're positioning content in the SERPs isn't correctly matching the intent behind search terms inputted by the user.

Keyword Position

Keyword rankings are a great way to measure the effectiveness of your efforts with SEO content.

Ranking in the number one (or position zero) SERP spot is the gold standard, if somewhat unattainable. It's also volatile because rankings change constantly depending on the specific user and their preferences as noted in the background by Google—plus the impact of future algorithm updates.

It's more realistic to aim for top 5 or 10 rankings. That said, anything ranking on the second page (positions 11–20) and beyond is unlikely to get many impressions and even less likely to achieve a decent CTR.

 **Chapter 20**

Style Guidance for Social Media

Although most of this style guide discusses long-form content, it's worth considering aspects of short-form social media content separately.

Many of the same rules still apply, but you have to adjust copy and visuals to what people expect on each social channel. You also need to consider people's shorter attention spans, as well as character count limitations on platforms like Twitter.

Although enterprise brands lead the charge when it comes to spending time putting together useful social brand guidelines, smaller businesses can also benefit from the effort. If you're working with a third party to run your brand's social media, you must give them a style guide to use—or collaborate in compiling one for them. That is essential: without it, you'll probably never be happy with the results. And you can't blame the third party for not getting your style right if you refuse to give them guidance.

Here are some special considerations to keep in mind when adapting your style guide for social media.

Brand Social Media Style Guide Examples

- **New York University (NYU)**[88]: NYU's social media style guide takes the time to go into very specific details regarding things like post timing and hashtag use, as well as how to write dates

---

[88] For more information, check out NYU's Social Media Style Guide:
https://www.nyu.edu/content/dam/nyu/cmsTeam/documents/socialmedia/NYU_SocialMedia_StyleGuide_092914.pdf

and times in a consistent way. It provides several useful examples to show what they want on brand social media channels.

- **Sprout Social**[89]: Sprout Social's social media style guide is presented in a fun, visual way that stays true to its branding. It's separated into three distinct sections: patterns, visuals, and writing. Contributors have a lot of guidance regarding the specific expectations of the brand.

- **University of North Carolina Greensboro (UNCG)**[90]: UNCG's social media style guide is fairly short, but it effectively covers all the most important details. It also offers screenshots of good and bad posts and multiple platform-specific examples.

Social Media Style Guide Sections

Your social media style guide will need some of the same sections as your long-form content style guide, but unless you're managing an enterprise brand with many different accounts, it shouldn't be as long or as detailed.

Here are the basic sections to consider including and building on:

- **Baseline style guide**: Should contributors revert to Associated Press (AP) style when a rule isn't explicitly defined? Which language and dialect are appropriate for a specific social account—for example, you may wish to specify US English versus UK English. For enterprise brands with multiple location-specific accounts, share language and style guidance as they change per account.

- **Specific profile links**: This is more or less administrative—creating a list with links to all the accounts associated with a

---

[89] You can find more on Sprout Social's style guide at: https://seeds.sproutsocial.com/
[90] University of North Carolina Greensboro has published its social media style guide online at: https://uc.uncg.edu/social-media-style-guide/

brand and any specific details that the social media manager should keep in mind.

- **Voice**: What distinguishes your brand from others in terms of your specific word choice and tone? That can be hard to define, but it's easier if you start by brainstorming the words you'd use to describe your brand if this wasn't something you'd thought about before. It's also helpful to compare your brand to other brands and how they communicate on social media. Ask yourself:
  - Is your brand snarky like the Wendy's Twitter account or more reserved like Sherwin-Williams' social presence?
  - Do you use funny GIFs or would your audience consider that unprofessional?
  - Don't forget to refer to the Nielsen Norman Group's spectrum of voice and tone dimensions introduced in Chapter 1.
- **Word choice**: Offer suggestions for how to share certain types of social posts that incorporate your brand's voice. It'll be even more helpful if you also share examples of acceptable jargon and words to avoid.
- **Punctuation**: If you're particular about using punctuation (like whether or not to use em-dashes and the Oxford comma), be sure to make that clear.
- **Competition**: It's helpful to create a list of your competitors so you can keep tabs on what they're doing—for example, to analyze what's working and what isn't—and then adjust your own efforts.
- **Audience details**: Share details about your audience with those creating content for the brand, including demographics, psychographics, other brands they like, and so on—the more details you provide, the better the results will be.

- **Goals**: What do you want your audience to do when engaging with your brand's social channels? Answering this question will help determine the call to action (CTA) text you use in the social copy. Take this a step further and suggest specific copy to use for CTAs. Note that, in general, social media is not a great place to directly make sales, so think more "top of the funnel" in terms of your goals and the copy you'll be using to get people to engage with your brand.

- **Using links**: Are there certain types of posts where links should be avoided (or shared as separate comments)? Make sure to state brand preferences in your social media style guide. Consider using a link shortener to increase brand awareness and make the link appear trustworthy—long links look spammy. You can also connect your **branded short link**[91] to a tool like JotURL for tracking purposes.

- **Post timing**: If you have any preferences or data regarding the best times to post or schedule content, it's worth adding this information here. Some social media scheduling tools, like Sprout Social, can help determine your brand's optimal post times per day and per network based on historical data.

- **How to use hashtags**: Each platform has unique rules, so share the best practices for each platform and describe where to place hashtags within the post copy (e.g., should they be on their own line?). Also, include a list of commonly used hashtags and use cases. If there's a branded hashtag that should be incorporated in certain posts, make sure to include guidelines for its use. As a best practice, share 1–2 hashtags per post (unless it's Instagram, in which case,

---

[91] A branded short link is the result of using a URL shortening tool (such as JotURL) in tandem with a custom branded domain (such as http://blgsmth.tips).

Instagram recommends using 3-5 hashtags per post).[92] Any more than that starts to look spammy.

- **Retweet/reshare/mentions policy**: Do you reshare content you're tagged in on social media? Do you acknowledge it with a reply? State brand preferences in your guide.
- **How to engage with others**: Create form responses for different situations. For example, what happens when a customer tags your social channels in an angry public rant? How about if someone uses a branded hashtag to share user-generated content (UGC)? Templates make it easier to respond in a timely manner but should be customized to the situation.
- **Crisis plan**: Social media is often the frontline for brands caught in controversy. As such, even if the brand is not at fault for being implicated in a bad situation, you should still create a crisis plan ahead of a possible crisis situation. If you're unsure where to start, look to other brands and how they've communicated with followers during a similar situation.
- **Employee social media guidelines**: Employees can be incredibly impactful when it comes to increasing engagement, but their association with your brand can also be damaging if social media guidelines aren't followed. Consider the following:
    - Do you have a preferred setup for how employees connect their profiles with your brand on social media (such as listing the brand as their employer)?
    - Do you have a preference for how they write a bio that incorporates your brand?

---

[92] Instagram's @Creators (@creators), "To Use or Not to Use Hashtags? Here's What You Need to Know + What You Should Avoid to Get the Most out of Adding Hashtags to Your Content ✔," Instagram photo, September 28, 2021, https://www.instagram.com/p/CUV20kxvLgS/.

- Do you have a preference for how they talk about your brand and share content on social media?

- **How to curate content**: Answer questions such as the following:
    - How often should you share curated content in addition to planned content?
    - What formatting rules apply to curated content? For example, should the social media manager tag the brand they're curating from?
    - What are your preferred sources for curating content (e.g., clients, partners, and non-competing brands)?

- **Visual guidelines**: Engaging visuals are of the utmost importance on social media, especially Instagram and Pinterest. If there are any graphics or templates you want social media managers to use, provide a cloud storage link to them for easy access. If you want your logo incorporated on some imagery (this is not recommended as a watermark on *all* imagery), provide some usage guidelines.

- **Emojis**: Answer questions such as the following:
    - Does your brand use emojis within posts?
    - How about when responding to followers?
    - Are there certain emojis you use in certain situations?

- **Themes**: This isn't about matters of style so much as helpful guidelines. Offer suggested themes to post about each day of the week. By specifying themes, you'll make it easier for a social media manager to create on-brand content that suits your goals. For example:
    - One day you share an industry tip.
    - Another day could have a curated article.
    - And yet another day may involve sharing a project you're working on.

- **Examples**: The most useful social media style guides share examples to illustrate each point. The more, the better.

Jump to the <u>Appendix</u> for access to The Blogsmith's social media style guide template.

It's certainly hard to come up with all these details when you're first starting out. It's better to create a working document that you can update as things come up or as you make decisions. For best results, experiment with theories and don't be afraid to change your stance over time.

Social media is an ever-changing medium. Even if your general style standards never change, you may have to update them for new social media platforms and features that your brand decides to use.

No matter what you choose to include in your social media style guide, the more detail and examples you can provide, the better your results when working with others. But, even for a one-person team, a style guide is helpful for staying consistent within your own efforts.

General Social Media Copywriting Guidelines

With your style guide sections defined, consider specifying general and network-specific style guidelines, such as these best practices:

- Don't overdo your sections with emojis.

For example:

"Maddy Osman operates The Blogsmith, an SEO content 🌐 agency 👩‍💻💻 for 📧 B2B tech 📱 companies 🏢 that works with clients 📔 like 🔖 HubSpot, Automattic, Kinsta, and Sprout 🌿 Social. 🧑‍💻👯 Maddy's background in ▢ WordPress web 🕸 design ✐ contributes to a well-rounded understanding 🌟 of SEO and how ▢ to connect brands 📅💬 to relevant search 🔎 prospects."

- Become familiar with slang or abbreviations that are unfamiliar. Use something like Urban Dictionary as a reference point if you're unsure of a term's meaning.
- Don't shorten words to comply with a character count unless it's a commonly recognized abbreviation that doesn't come across as unprofessional.
- Don't sacrifice important rules of grammar to meet a character count. That said, sometimes you can use symbols instead of words where it makes sense (e.g., "%" instead of "percent").
- Use sentence case (only the first word and proper nouns capitalized)—not title case (all major words [4+ letters] capitalized). Title case is way too hard to read as a sentence.

For example:

Don't write this:	Write this instead:
"Does Your SEO Word Count Matter in Content Creation? Find Out if It Does and How You Can Take Advantage of It in Your Blog Articles."	*"Does your SEO word count matter in content creation? Find out if it does and how you can take advantage of it in your blog articles."*

There's a reason it's called *title* case.

- **What do you want someone to do after reading the copy?** Tell them with a CTA. Whenever possible, create urgency for action (even if you don't provide a reason for the urgency).

For example:

"Read the article: [article URL]"

- **Use hard returns to add white space**. That will make your copy more readable and, therefore, actionable.

Aiming for two separate short paragraphs is a good goal for the average tweet. Add the CTA to the end of the second paragraph.

Although the character count is much more flexible on Facebook and LinkedIn, it's best to keep social posts below three separate short paragraphs. If you feel like sharing more information about a specific topic, consider turning it into long-form content (e.g., a blog post).

- **Make sure that the combination of your copy and visuals sets clear expectations for what someone will encounter after clicking through**. Don't use empty clickbait headings.
- **Quotes, statistics, and examples** are some of the most compelling social media copy.
- **Use a curiosity gap to create tension**.[93]
- **Use copy to invite a response**. People love being asked for their opinion.
- **Describe benefits, not features**.

For example:

Don't write this:	Write this instead:
"AirPod Pros offer silicone tips in three sizes, "Hey Siri" support, and IPX4 water and sweat resistance."	"AirPod Pros are a powerful combination headphone/microphone that you can use for almost any situation."

- **Use numbers to set expectations**. Whether to quantify the number of items in an article or describe the length of video content, using numbers gives social media users an idea of what to expect from the content you're sharing.

---

[93] Ben Sailer, "How to Use Curiosity Gaps to Create Tension and Keep Customer's Attention For as Long as You Want With Andrew Davis [AMP 169]," *CoSchedule* (blog), January 28, 2020, https://coschedule.com/blog/how-to-use-curiosity-gaps-to-create-tension-and-keep-customers-attention-for-as-long-as-you-want-with-andrew-davis-amp-169.

Social Network-Specific Guidelines

Here are some basic guidelines to adapt style for social media communications.

Instagram

- Hide hashtags in comments to create clean-looking captions.
- Plan around the fact that you have no clickable links—except your profile link and within Stories. You can use tools like SleekBio to add a link tree to your clickable profile link.
- Specify your account's color scheme or specific filters to use for cohesion. The quality of your visuals is important for getting attention, while copy can help you push someone towards a specific action.
- Designate and share a specific hashtag on your website (OK) or in your social profile bio (best) that customers can use to submit UGC.

Twitter

- Use 1–2 hashtags, at most—ideally after the copy and URL, and never as the first word in the post. If it looks spammy to you, it will definitely look spammy to your audience. As a starting point, check out the brand's Twitter channel for common hashtags used.
- **Add relevant handles or names wherever possible**. At a minimum, on Twitter, add the @handle of the brand that created the content you're sharing. If possible, add the author's name (if shared on the article)/@handle (if they have a Twitter account). It may also be appropriate to create social media content mentioning contributors' names/@handles (such as with an expert roundup) or brands/sources mentioned in the content.

For example:

"Wondering what to send in an order confirmation email? Learn from #ecommerce success stories such as @cocoandeve, @AppSumo, @everyplate (+ 3 more brands) on @MailPoet's guide to first purchase emails:

https://www.mailpoet.com/blog/first-purchase-emails-to-create-loyal-customers/"

- Don't automate anything in terms of sending messages or replying to tweets. It's easy to see through and people resent it. Communicating on social networks like Twitter is a good example of where style and etiquette intersect.

LinkedIn

- Don't overdo it with **broetry**, a series of short paragraphs. Carina Rampelt further characterizes broetry as having a "clickbait opener, cliché ending, and emotionally charged anecdote."[94]

For example:

Broetry may seem compelling. Rodney certainly thought so.

And all the white space between each one-line paragraph is nice for a bit.

But it's too much of a good thing. The lack of formatting diversity gets old, fast.

His boss started to see his preference for broetry as a weakness (and it was).

Rodney was fired from his job as a copywriter.

But when one door closes, another opens.

Rodney had paved the way for his true calling as a clown.

---

[94] Carina Rampelt, "Why You Should Avoid the Broetry Writing Trend," *Content Marketing Institute* (blog), accessed March 9, 2022, https://contentmarketinginstitute.com/2020/11/avoid-broetry-writing-trend/.

- Add links in comments (not post copy) to improve post reach.
- Personalize a connection request, even just to say where you met the person or why you want to connect with *them* specifically.

Pinterest

In many ways, Pinterest search engine optimization (SEO) is like long-form content SEO. Both involve the use of keywords in key signal areas.

Pinterest visuals are very influential in catching attention that leads to action. As a rule, you'll want to use vertical imagery or videos for the best results on this platform.[95]

Here are some basic rules about Pinterest style and adjusting for robot search spiders.

There are essentially three places you can add keywords to help your ideal audience find you on Pinterest:

- Pinterest account description.
- Pinterest board title and description.
- Pin description.

Pinterest Account Description

The **Pinterest account description** is the description to summarize the nature of your account. It appears on your main Pinterest profile page.

---

[95] "Make Pins That Perform," Pinterest, accessed March 9, 2022, https://business.pinterest.com/en/creative-best-practices/.

About The Blogsmith ✕

🌐 **the-blogsmith.com**

+👤 **7k followers** · 188.3k monthly views

👥 **475 following** **Account Keyword**

Maddy Osman is The Blogsmith, focused on SEO writing for clients like GoDaddy, AAA, BigCommerce, & Automattic. She shares lessons learned on: The-Blogsmith.com

Figure 20.1 Pinterest account description, incorporating the account keyword "*SEO writing*."

Pinterest Board Title and Description

The **Pinterest board title and description** is the label for a specific category of your pins and a longer description about the category.

Pinterest Board description template:

- Repeat the board title (it's the same as the board keyword).
- Incorporate the account keyword (if relevant).

Figure 20.2 A Pinterest board description that incorporates "*WordPress SEO tips*" as the primary keyword.[96]

For example:

Board title: "***WordPress SEO tips***"

Board description: "***WordPress SEO tips*** *that help The Blogsmith optimize for technical SEO, onsite SEO, and building backlinks.*"

Pin Description

The **Pin description** is the description for a specific pin within a particular Pinterest board.

Pin description template:

- Write a unique Pin description.
- Incorporate the account keyword.
- Incorporate the board keyword.
- Add a link to your homepage (explain its purpose).
- Write a compelling and specific CTA.

---

[96] Maddy Osman, "WordPress SEO Tips," Pinterest Board, accessed March 9, 2022, https://www.pinterest.com/maddyosman/wordpress-seo-tips/.

Figure 20.3 A Pin description for "The Budget Guide to Bangkok Thailand."[97]

For example:

"*Bangkok Thailand (unique description) --- Tanks that Get Around* **is an online store** *(website's purpose) offering a selection of* **funny travel clothes** *(account keyword) for world explorers.*

Check out **www.tanksthatgetaround.com** *for funny travel tank tops (CTA) and more* **Thailand travel guides** *and* **budget travel tips** *(board keywords)."*

Facebook

It's difficult to get results on Facebook without ad spend. Regardless, you should maintain a consistent and responsive professional presence. Essentially, you don't want your Facebook page to look like an abandoned storefront with unanswered comments or days between new content.

---

[97] Tanks that Get Around, "The Budget Guide to Bangkok Thailand," Pin, Pinterest, July 11, 2017, https://www.pinterest.com/pin/647251777706008113/.

Pro tip:

If you're using a social media scheduler, you can copy your LinkedIn post over to Facebook as a general rule.

 **Chapter 21**

How to Create Your Brand Style Guide

Few things work perfectly straight out of the box for every use case. That is why many software tools include the option to use custom fields.

Foundational style guidelines are no different. While they're a great starting point, they rarely account for your or other brand's preferences.

For example, you may adopt certain spellings or prefer a word over others depending on your industry.

Let's take the word *"site."* While it sufficiently describes an online entity, The Blogsmith Style Guide stipulates you should spell it out as *"website"* to add specificity.

To get precisely what you want out of specific content, you'll need to customize these guidelines to fit your needs. Use these ideas as inspiration for creating your own custom style rules.

The Associated Press (AP) Stylebook and Other Popular Style Guides

The *AP Stylebook* is considered the gold standard for public-facing corporate communications. It covers many use cases, from preferred spelling and grammar rules to agreement issues, capitalization, and formatting.

Many different professions, including public relations (PR), defer to the *AP Stylebook* for communications. As such, it's a commonly understood "language" for content creation. It simplifies the process of getting your content team to reach an agreement on basic communication standards.

Depending on the nature of the topics your web content covers, you can still reference other style guides, such as the following:

- *The Chicago Manual of Style* (**CMOS**), which is commonly used in book publishing.
- *The Modern Language Association Handbook* (**MLA**), which is commonly used in academia.
- *Publication Manual of the American Psychological Association* (**APA**), which is commonly used in psychology, sociology, politics, and education.

It's important to note that news journalism and online content writing have many differences. This is why many brands that invest in content creation build their own style guides based on AP style. Traditional news publications maintain their own in-house style guides that also work in tandem with AP style.

Drawing Inspiration from Other Brand Style Guides

It's going to take a significant amount of time to develop a distinct style guide for your brand. After all, it's hard to understand your brand preferences without working through specific situations and determining if you want to create a rule for handling each of them in the future.

And even when you think you've been exposed to all possible situations and your style guide is a bulletproof resource, you'll encounter something new you never had to consider before. Once you figure out how to handle this new situation, you'll need to update your style guide accordingly.

There's a reason why the *AP Stylebook* is typically updated every two years—things change! Society changes. Rules, too, must change. Even in between major guide releases, editors address questions of style not explicitly defined in the *AP Stylebook* in the weekly "Ask the Editors" updates.

But don't let the prospect of an everlasting project deter you from trying.

Besides using the *AP Stylebook* as a foundation, you can also draw inspiration from the following brands that have thoughtfully developed and defined their brand style over time:

- **Mailchimp**: If you're looking for the ideal, well-rounded brand style guide, look no further. Mailchimp's brand styles focus on a whole lot more than just content. Something like this is an incredible asset a brand can share with a vendor to quickly get them up to speed.

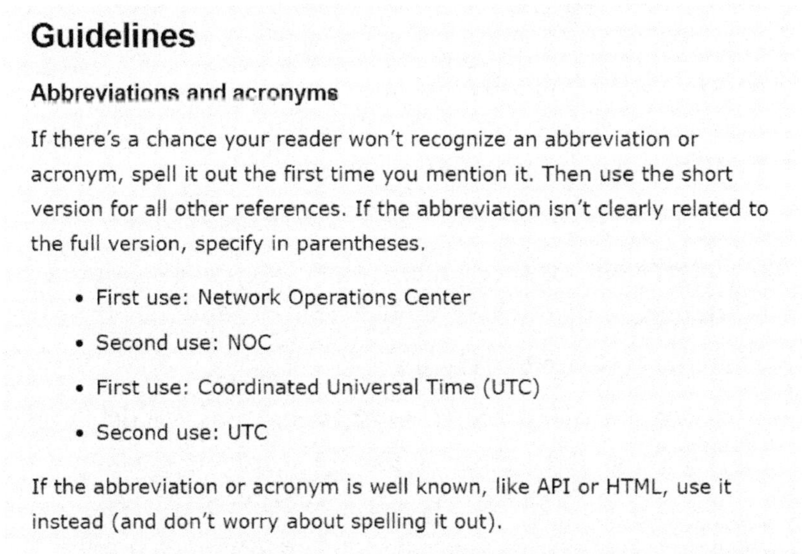

Guidelines

Abbreviations and acronyms

If there's a chance your reader won't recognize an abbreviation or acronym, spell it out the first time you mention it. Then use the short version for all other references. If the abbreviation isn't clearly related to the full version, specify in parentheses.

- First use: Network Operations Center
- Second use: NOC
- First use: Coordinated Universal Time (UTC)
- Second use: UTC

If the abbreviation or acronym is well known, like API or HTML, use it instead (and don't worry about spelling it out).

Figure 21.1 Mailchimp's style guide discussing how to use abbreviations and acronyms.[98]

- **Orbit Media**: This style guide offers useful template guidelines for inviting guest contributors to submit on-brand

[98] "Grammar and Mechanics | Mailchimp Content Style Guide," Mailchimp, accessed March 9, 2022, https://styleguide.mailchimp.com/grammar-and-mechanics/.

guest posts for your blog. Also, make sure to read their style guide's **preferred words** section.

Orbit preferred words:

- call to action (no hyphens)

- Domain Authority (always capitalized)

- e words in general (lower case, no hyphen)

- ecommerce (lower case, no hyphen)

- thank you page (no hyphen)

- internet (lower case)

- homepage (one word, no hyphen)

Figure 21.2 Orbit Media's style guide showing their preferred words.[99]

- **BuzzFeed**: This style guide goes as far as sharing a preferred dictionary that writers should reference (besides their own) for correct or approved spelling.

There are many important considerations for timely news reporting that other types of content creators don't necessarily need to worry about. Notably, at least five specific bullet points are dedicated to ampersand style. If you appreciate great attention to detail, you'll love BuzzFeed's style guide.

---

[99] "Orbit Guest Blogging Guidelines," Orbit Media Studios, accessed March 9, 2022, https://www.orbitmedia.com/guidelines/.

Grammar, Spelling, and Punctuation Guidelines

Ampersands

• Generally do not use spaces on either side of ampersands in constructions like Q&A, R&B, etc.

• NEVER use a serial comma before an ampersand.

• Don't use an ampersand as a stand-in for and in headlines or running copy.

• If using ampersands in recipe names, be consistent with their use throughout a post.

• Adhere to self-stylization for companies, titles, etc., that use an ampersand.

Figure 21.3 BuzzFeed's style guide discussing proper usage of ampersands.[100]

- **A List Apart**: This style guide offers useful guidelines for blogs that share code samples. It's worth reading regardless of your niche because it's simple and to the point.

CODE BLOCKS

Please use tab for line indentation. Each nested line is indented one tab from the parent.

Control structures such as parentheses require spacing on the outside only:

```
if (foo  bar) {
  // do something
}
```

Figure 21.4 A List Apart's style guide discussing code blocks.[101]

---

[100] Emmy Favilla and Buzzfeed News, "BuzzFeed Style Guide," BuzzFeed, March 3, 2022, https://www.buzzfeed.com/emmyf/buzzfeed-style-guide.
[101] "Style Guide," A List Apart, March 25, 2019, https://alistapart.com/about/style-guide/.

- **Google Developer Documentation Style Guide**: This style guide provides useful guidance for technical writing with numerous examples. It's a great style foundation for software as a service (SaaS) companies and other brands trying to use content to break down complex ideas. It also addresses topic-specific questions such as, "When should I use a table?"

List or table?

Tables and lists are both ways to present a set of similarly structured items; sometimes it's not obvious when to choose one presentation over the other. To decide which presentation to use, consult the following table:

Item type	Example	How to present
Each item is a single unit.	A list of programming language names, or a list of steps to follow.	Use a numbered list, lettered list, or bulleted list.
Each item is a pair of pieces of related data.	A list of term/definition pairs.	Use a description list (or, in some contexts, a table).
Each item is three or more pieces of related data.	A set of parameters, where each parameter has a name, a data type, and a description.	Use a table.

Figure 21.5 Google Developer Documentation Style Guide highlighting when to use a table.[102]

- **Microsoft**: This style guide focuses on sharing details for innovative features the company has created for customers (such as chatbots). A notable inclusion related to online content writing is a section on creating responsive (mobile) content.

  An underlying company mission of creating accessible technology also means there's guidance to help developers effectively communicate complex ideas to diverse users.

[102] "Tables | Google Developer Documentation Style Guide," Google Developers, February 28, 2022, https://developers.google.com/style/tables.

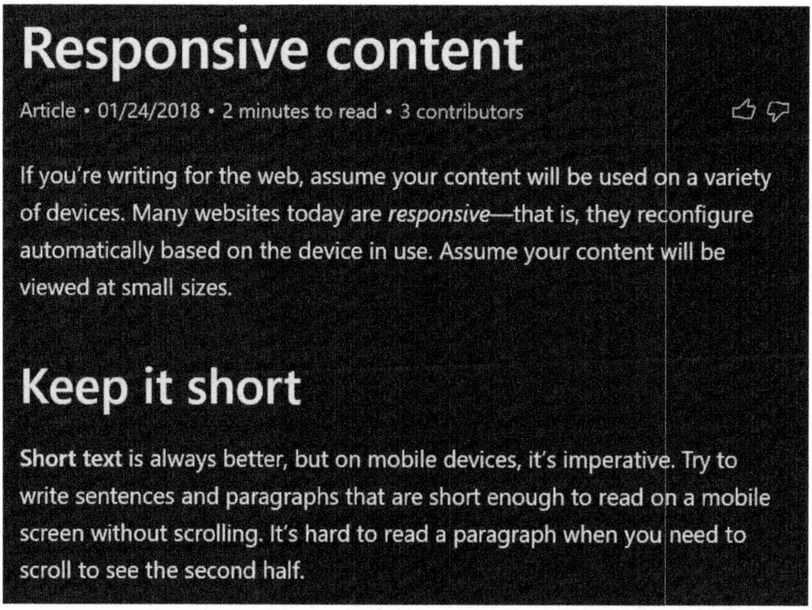

Responsive content

Article • 01/24/2018 • 2 minutes to read • 3 contributors   👍 👎

If you're writing for the web, assume your content will be used on a variety of devices. Many websites today are *responsive*—that is, they reconfigure automatically based on the device in use. Assume your content will be viewed at small sizes.

Keep it short

Short text is always better, but on mobile devices, it's imperative. Try to write sentences and paragraphs that are short enough to read on a mobile screen without scrolling. It's hard to read a paragraph when you need to scroll to see the second half.

Figure 21.6 Microsoft's style guide describing how to optimize content for mobile devices.[103]

- **Atlassian**: This style guide notably includes guidelines for inclusive language, making its recommendations useful across the various global enterprise teams that depend on Atlassian's popular apps to do business. Atlassian also offers specific guidelines to write copy for app notifications and features. Additionally, its efforts to share specifics of voice and tone include helpful visuals for getting important/on-brand points across.

---

[103] pallep, v-anpasi, and camind, "Responsive Content - Microsoft Style Guide," Microsoft Docs, January 24, 2018, https://docs.microsoft.com/en-us/style-guide/responsive-content.

Our stance on inclusive language

The words we choose are the building blocks and the glue that hold our diverse teams together. Language not only has the power to build bridges and increase understanding, but also the capability to alienate and dismiss.

At Atlassian, our diverse teams build tools for an equally diverse audience, and we strive to use inclusive language in all we do. We know that, as a society, we are always evolving and the language we use must also evolve. This influences how we build things and how we communicate — both internally and externally. We encourage ourselves to seek first to understand the impact of our words, intentional or unintentional, and we diligently reexamine our word choices as we all learn and grow.

Figure 21.7 Atlassian's style guide discussing the company's stance on inclusive language.[104]

Style Guide Sections

After taking some time to understand AP style and gather inspiration from the style guides of established brands, you're ready to start defining the various sections that will make up your own brand's rule book.

Here are some common considerations regarding what to include:

- A backup style guide (such as the *AP Stylebook*) for content creators to reference if a rule isn't explicitly defined in your brand's rule book.
- Mission statements and goals for your content.
- Relevant audience information.
- Technical requirements (such as average word count and punctuation specifics).
- Perspective (first, second, third person).
- Image guidelines (such as a minimum width for resolution).
- Submission guidelines (such as who to send submissions to).

---

[104] "Inclusive Language," Atlassian Design System, accessed March 9, 2022, https://atlassian.design/content/inclusive-writing.

- Attribution guidelines (e.g., should contributors share a headshot, bio, or social media links?).
- Ownership and republishing rights (such as for guest posting).
- Brand style information for graphic creation (such as logos, colors, typography).
- Correct spellings of branded terms for easy reference (think of this as your public-facing PR media kit).
- Voice/tone (how *you* say things and refer to *yourselves*).
- How you measure success.
- Important text formatting specifics.
- Popular posts (to help creators visualize what success looks like).

Jump to the Appendix for a blank style guide template.

Updating Your Brand Style Guide

Your first attempt at creating a style guide is just a rough draft for what it will eventually become. Once you share your style guide with content creators on your team, you'll be presented consistently with new situations for defining style.

Thus, your style guide is a working document that should be updated regularly. Just as important, you need to make it easy for your team to be alerted regarding new changes so they don't continue to make the same style errors. For repeated style guide infractions, content editors should share comments reminding content creators of the specific style guide rule they're violating.

On a related note, a style guide isn't a replacement for a human editor. Just because you take the time to set rules doesn't necessarily mean that your team will commit them to memory. That said, a style guide makes it easier for editors to do their job because it exists to set expectations for all content creation efforts.

Some brands, including those shared earlier in this chapter, create public-facing versions of their style guides. Some take this a step further and publish a hybrid document that has both public-facing and private sections only visible to certain logged-in users (Atlassian is a great example of this).

This page is restricted to Atlassian employees

To view this page, you must be an Atlassian employee and log in with your Atlassian account. If you are logged in and still having trouble, contact the Atlassian Design System team.

Contact us

Figure 21.8 Atlassian has restricted sections in their online style guide only available to its employees.[105]

You should keep your style guide private for internal use—at least in the initial development stages—unless there's a compelling reason to make it public. For example, if you accept third-party content contributions (such as guest blog posts), you may want to make your style guide public to set easily accessible expectations for content you define as worthy of publication. Alternatively, you could create and offer a pared-down version of your internal style guide for this

---

[105] "Overview - Content," Atlassian Design System, accessed March 9, 2022, https://atlassian.design/content/vocabulary/.

purpose.

Where to store your style guide documentation? If it's meant to be available to external parties, Google Docs is a great solution. If it's meant to be available only to internal team members, an intranet with access control, like Notion, may be a more fitting alternative.

On Google Docs, you can share your style guide document with each member of your team and leave comments that will notify each shared member whenever new changes are made. Break down guidance into easily scannable sections so your team doesn't have to work too hard to reference specific guidelines. Add a clickable table of contents to further aid ease of use.

Jump Ahead to a Specific Section:

Content Agency. Behind the Scenes

Freelancers: Behind the Scenes

Considerations When Outsourcing to Agencies vs. Freelancers

Freelancer vs. Agency — The Advantages and Disadvantages of Hiring

Why Choose an Agency Over a Freelancer

What To Look For When Hiring an Agency

Final Thoughts: Agency vs. Freelancer — The Differences for Content Creation

Figure 21.9 A clickable table of contents in a published article for The Blogsmith. [106]

---

106 Maddy Osman, "The Difference Between Working With an Agency vs. Freelancer for Content Creation," The Blogsmith, February 3, 2022, https://www.theblogsmith.com/agency-vs-freelancer-outsource-content-writing/.

 Chapter 22

Further Reading

This style guide is but one resource to consider in the pursuit of creating great content and being a better communicator. In order to define a unique style, you must consider additional perspectives from additional angles.

Here are some essential books and guides to read for developing a preferred writing style and technique for your brand.

Figure 22.1 Further reading to develop your writing style.

The Elements of Style

If you read one resource on this list, let this be it. It's an essential grammar guide for writers of any medium. *The Elements of Style* by William Strunk Jr. and E.B. White was first published in 1919, but many of the rules it shares still hold true today. Use it as a foundation from which to build your own style guide.

The Associated Press Stylebook

The Associated Press Stylebook isn't necessarily meant to be read through like a book, but you should keep a copy close at hand as a reference point when developing best practices. An updated print copy, which you can buy as a spiral-bound notebook, is published every other year in the spring. Alternatively, or in addition to the print copy, digital access is a convenient and affordable option.

Google's Search Quality Rater Guidelines

Google's Search Quality Rater Guidelines are standards shared by Google with Quality Raters. This role exists to evaluate search results based on meeting searchers' needs and sharing high-quality information. At 172 pages long in the 2021 edition, it's by no means a quick read. Even so, it's worth the time for the gems it contains about understanding how Google develops its algorithm.

The Adweek Copywriting Handbook

Check out *The Adweek Copywriting Handbook* by Joseph Sugarman for guidance around improving copy and making it more compelling. Copywriting combines marketing and writing, with a focus on encouraging consumers to take certain desired actions. When it comes to content writing, being a good copywriter can help improve headings, flow, and—ultimately—conversions.

On Writing

Stephen King is a legendary fiction writer who is notorious for pumping out a ridiculous amount of writing in a short space of time. He has published hundreds of stories throughout his life, with new titles being released on a regular basis.

He's a deeply engaging storyteller who knows how to grab readers' interest and keep them hooked across hundreds of pages. Read *On Writing* as part King "memoir" and part "how-to guide" for emulating his writing style and process.

CONCLUSION

The End and the Beginning

At this point, you've read a lot about style and important aspects of the content creation process. You've learned about the distinctions and similarities between writing for humans and robots. You've dug deep into specifics like list and link formatting and how to incorporate effective visuals with written copy.

After working with dozens of discerning editors throughout my freelance writing career, I've learned a lot from the standards of each brand they represent and have shared some of the best takeaways throughout this book. These lessons learned over many years of trial, error, and the experience of those wiser than me, are reflected on every page.

If you've read this far, you've learned all about my style rules. And now it's time to create your own.

Here's why it's worth the time (if I haven't convinced you yet!):

In general, members of your content team will continue to make the same style mistakes if they're not able to articulate a specific guideline. A detailed style guide ensures that everyone on your team is in agreement about the best way to do something. Creating guidelines helps to cut wasteful time spent on the same words, phrases, and grammar constructs being written, and then edited or deleted—over and over again.

That's why it's valuable to codify the rules.

Experiment with some ideas you haven't tried yet to see if they improve the reading experience and your most important key performance indicators (KPIs). Try adapting any ideas that aren't an exact fit but that you can mold to be. Make your brand style truly distinctive as you figure out what it is over time.

With all that said, I'm not saying that my style guide should look exactly like yours. But both should start from a similar foundation. Specifically, regardless of who you're writing for, make sure to focus on the reader experience. While you're at it, make sure that you're formatting content so that robots have enough context to recommend it to your target reader when they seek it out.

Creating thoughtful, well-constructed content shows a high commitment to providing the best experience for your reader. Reading through this guide is just the first step. What you do with it determines its usefulness to your content efforts.

Maddy Osman, Founder of The Blogsmith

ACKNOWLEDGMENTS

I started this book in the winter of 2020, after a rough few years of loss and grief. I wrote this book during NaNoWriMo, which is short for "National Novel Writing Month." NaNoWriMo is a yearly event in November where participants work on a book project with a goal of writing 50,000 words in 30 days.

This book wouldn't be here, in this form, without lots of input from people I trust. Anyone who thinks they could write, polish, and launch a book completely by themselves isn't doing everything they can to create something truly great for their intended audience.

Given the time commitment to produce the required amount of copy, my first acknowledgment is to my husband, Dan French, who helped pick up a lot of my slack during the month of November 2020 (and then again when I went through edits!). I was on the brink of starting my own business when we first met. At the point that I was ready to make the jump, Dan supported my choices from the earliest unknowns. I love that he's always believed in me, and the feeling is mutual. He gives me the space to pursue my passions.

Thanks to Dan's family, who have always welcomed me with open arms and taken an interest in my various projects. And thanks to my family for always encouraging me to follow my dreams while serving as role models for professionalism.

Next, I have to thank my mom, Kathy Osman, a former English teacher. She has always been a role model for proper language and grammar, so I asked her to do a first run-through to edit my book. She helped me understand where specialized concepts could use more explanation and other holes in my own biased logic. It most certainly was a labor of love.

Although he's no longer here to read this acknowledgment, big thanks are due to my dad, John Osman—may he rest in peace. My dad has always been a role model for entrepreneurship and has never doubted that I could grow up to be whatever I wanted. He's always supported me along the path, and I miss him every day. I strive to make you proud of the woman I'm becoming.

Every member of The Blogsmith team has contributed to this book in some meaningful way because they're all committed to our purpose of creating high-quality, useful content.

Specifically, I want to recognize:

- Ren Rauland and Stephanie Holland for having a big impact on developing style.
- Diego Trejo and Ammar Qazi for continuing to refine and defend our style—contributing many concepts that helped shape these guidelines.
- Amanda Moutinho for holding up issues of style and process against the lens of our clients' unique needs.
- Jasmine Leechuy, who is amazing to work with in general. She makes our style better by being thoughtful, thorough, and asking questions.
- Farrah Garcia, who is one of the best researchers I've met and who helped fact-check aspects of this book.
- Rochelle Serapion for her help developing The Blogsmith's approach to SEO content.

Each of these individuals has helped me see the world in a different way, and I'm better for it.

Thanks to my best friends, in order of when I met them: Nicole Prusinski, Kayla Knoll, and Samm Mammoser. Each of you has always made me feel like I could achieve any goal I set. I'm proud to be surrounded by such bad-ass broads. Shout out to my best dude friend, Zack Wilmot, for all your friendship and support since our teenage years.

Anne Abel Smith is due thanks for her professional edits, which helped create a more consistent structure for each section and feature. I must also express my gratitude to everyone in my mastermind groups who provided feedback at different stages of the writing and promotion process: Ana Cvetkovic, Caitlin Fitzpatrick, Erin Flynn, Joe Casabona, and Brian Richards.

I want to thank my mentors who have published books—some that I've helped launch! Marti Konstant, Barbara Schultz, Jeff Hyman, and Daniel G. Newman.

Thanks to Vernon Southward's team at Easelly (shout out to Jonas Arellano for all your help!). They helped put together many images to better communicate concepts for this book. They also handle much of The Blogsmith's client design needs. And thank you to Design Pickle, who also helped with book visuals and ongoing client designs.

Thanks to all my online friends (especially the WordPress community!) for following along and encouraging me when I shared NaNoWriMo updates.

There are many more people who have made major impacts on me, and ultimately this book. If you think I'm talking about you, I probably am. Thank you for being a part of my life.

It certainly takes a village, even for a self-published book! Finally, thanks to you, reader—you give all the hard work meaning.

BIBLIOGRAPHY

Creative Commons. "About The Licenses." Accessed March 10, 2022. https://creativecommons.org/licenses/.

Associated Press Stylebook. "AP Stylebook: Contractions." Accessed March 7, 2022. https://www.apstylebook.com/ap_stylebook/contractions.

Associated Press Stylebook. "AP Stylebook: Months." Accessed March 17, 2022. https://www.apstylebook.com/ap_stylebook/months.

Associated Press Stylebook. "AP Stylebook: Percent, Percentage, Percentage Points." Accessed March 17, 2022. https://www.apstylebook.com/ap_stylebook/percent-percentage-percentage-points.

Associated Press Stylebook. "Ask the Editor: Beginning a Sentence with a Conjunction." Accessed March 7, 2022. https://www.apstylebook.com/ask_the_editors/25415.

Associated Press Stylebook. "Ask the Editor: Should a Sentence End with a Preposition?" Accessed March 7, 2022. https://www.apstylebook.com/ask_the_editors/41877.

Bradt, George. "Wanamaker Was Wrong -- The Vast Majority Of Advertising Is Wasted." Forbes, September 14, 2016. https://www.forbes.com/sites/georgebradt/2016/09/14/wanamaker-was-wrong-the-vast-majority-of-advertising-is-wasted/.

Carnegie, Dale. *How to Win Friends and Influence People*. United States: Simon & Schuster, 1936.

Cavagnetto, Stacey. "How to Create a Blog Post That Gets Results." Koozai, October 16, 2020. https://www.koozai.com/blog/content-marketing-seo/anatomy-perfect-blog-post/.

Google. "Data Retention - Analytics Help." Accessed March 9, 2022. https://support.google.com/analytics/answer/7667196?hl=en.

Doran, George T. "There's a S.M.A.R.T. Way to Write Management's Goals and Objectives." *Management Review* 70, no. 11 (1981): 35–36.

Google. "Search Quality Rater Guidelines." Google, October 19, 2021. https://static.googleusercontent.com/media/guidelines.raterhub.com/en//searchqualityevaluatorguidelines.pdf.

Grammarly. "How Long Is a Paragraph?," April 6, 2017. https://www.grammarly.com/blog/how-long-is-a-paragraph/.

Neil Patel. "How to Write Headlines: A Step-by-Step Guide," August 25, 2021. https://neilpatel.com/blog/the-step-by-step-guide-to-writing-powerful-headlines/.

Hung, Wilson. "Content Marketing Analytics: What We Learned Analyzing 650,000 Hits." Sumo, November 2, 2018. https://sumo.com/stories/how-many-visitors-read-article.

Huxley, Aldous. *Brave New World*. United Kingdom: Chatto & Windus, 1932.

Instagram's @Creators (@creators). "To Use or Not to Use Hashtags? Here's What You Need to Know + What You Should Avoid to Get the Most out of Adding Hashtags to Your Content ✔." Instagram photo, September 28, 2021. https://www.instagram.com/p/CUV20kxvLgS/.

Jeffers, Jackie. "Study: The Readability of Your Website Is Affecting Your Conversion Rates." Portent, November 17, 2020. https://www.portent.com/blog/cro/study-the-readability-of-your-website-is-affecting-your-conversion-rates.htm.

Keysar, Dvir, and Tomer Shmiel. Question answering using entity references in unstructured data. United States US20160371385A1, filed August 30, 2016, and issued December 22, 2016. https://patents.google.com/patent/US20160371385/en.

King, Stephen. *On Writing: A Memoir of the Craft*. 1st ed. Scribner, 2000.

Lee, Kevan. "How to Perform an A/B Test on Your Website." Buffer, April 10, 2014. https://buffer.com/resources/how-buffer-ab-tests/.

Pinterest. "Make Pins That Perform." Accessed March 9, 2022. https://business.pinterest.com/en/creative-best-practices/.

Mcknight, Travis. "Study: How Content Readability Affects SEO and Rankings." Portent, June 17, 2021. https://www.portent.com/blog/content/study-how-content-readability-affects-seo-and-rankings.htm.

Moz. "Meta Description." Accessed March 17, 2022. https://moz.com/learn/seo/meta-description.

Montti, Roger. "Why Google Ranks Singular and Plural Keywords Differently." Search Engine Journal, June 30, 2020. https://www.searchenginejournal.com/singular-plural-keywords-google/373297/.

Moran, Kate. "The Four Dimensions of Tone of Voice." Nielsen Norman Group, 2016. https://www.nngroup.com/articles/tone-of-voice-dimensions/.

Moz. "Moz Pro Pricing." Accessed March 11, 2022. https://moz.com/products/pro/pricing.

Nayak, Pandu. "Understanding Searches Better than Ever Before." Google, October 25, 2019.

https://blog.google/products/search/search-language-understanding-bert/.

Neil Patel. "Ultimate Headline Formula List." Neil Patel, 2020. https://neilpatel.com/wp-content/uploads/2020/05/ultimate-headline-formula-list.pdf.

Ogilvy, David. *Ogilvy on Advertising*. 1st ed. Vintage, 1985.

Osman, Maddy. "Top 10 User Engagement KPIs to Measure." Search Engine Journal, February 3, 2019. https://www.searchenginejournal.com/content-marketing-kpis/user-engagement-metrics/.

Ahrefs. "Plans & Pricing." Accessed March 11, 2022. https://ahrefs.com/pricing.

Merriam-Webster. "Prepositions, Ending a Sentence With," 2019. https://www.merriam-webster.com/words-at-play/prepositions-ending-a-sentence-with.

Rampelt, Carina. "Why You Should Avoid the Broetry Writing Trend." *Content Marketing Institute* (blog). Accessed March 9, 2022. https://contentmarketinginstitute.com/2020/11/avoid-broetry-writing-trend/.

Sailer, Ben. "How to Use Curiosity Gaps to Create Tension and Keep Customer's Attention For as Long as You Want With Andrew Davis [AMP 169]." *CoSchedule* (blog), January 28, 2020. https://coschedule.com/blog/how-to-use-curiosity-gaps-to-create-tension-and-keep-customers-attention-for-as-long-as-you-want-with-andrew-davis-amp-169.

Yoast. "The Flesch Reading Ease Score: Why and How to Use It," May 20, 2019. https://yoast.com/flesch-reading-ease-score/.

University of Chicago Press. *The Chicago Manual of Style*. 16th ed. Chicago: University of Chicago Press, 2010.

Hotjar. "What Is a Sales Funnel? Why It's Important + How to Build

Yours," January 25, 2022. https://www.hotjar.com/conversion-rate-optimization/glossary/sales-funnel/.

BrightEdge. "What Is a Search Engine Spider?" Accessed March 9, 2022. https://www.brightedge.com/glossary/search-engine-spiders.

Wiebe, Joanna. "5 Landing Page Headline Formulas You Can Test Today." Unbounce, January 14, 2013. https://unbounce.com/landing-pages/5-headline-formulas/.

"How to Engage with the Bucket Brigade Technique." Copyhackers, October 3, 2017. https://copyhackers.com/engage-bucket-brigade-technique/.

"Should You Use a Curiosity Gap to Persuade Your Visitors to Click?" Copyhackers, April 15, 2014. https://copyhackers.com/2014/04/curiosity-gap/.

"The Ultimate Guide to No-Pain Copywriting (or, Every Copywriting Formula Ever)." Copyhackers, October 28, 2015. https://copyhackers.com/2015/10/copywriting-formula/.

APPENDIX

Resources

Please note: some of the following links are affiliate links, which means I'll receive a commission if you sign up using them. I've used the products and services recommended below.

General Writing Tools

- **Grammarly** (http://blgsmth.tips/grammarly): A spelling and grammar checking tool that integrates with Google Docs. The Blogsmith uses Grammarly's style guide feature.
- **Help a Report Out (HARO)** (http://blgsmth.tips/haro): A free service matching journalists with expert sources. Sign up for their thrice daily email, with queries organized by industry.
- **How to Establish an Efficient Process for Running Expert Roundups** (http://blgsmth.tips/expert-roundups): The Blogsmith's process for writing an expert roundup article.
- **How to Submit a HARO Query That Gets High-Quality Results** (http://blgsmth.tips/haro-tips): The Blogsmith's advice for submitting useful HARO queries.
- **Databox Blog** (http://blgsmth.tips/databox): Excellent examples of expert roundups to use as a reference point.
- **Google Forms** (http://blgsmth.tips/google-forms): A free tool for collecting feedback and other details. The Blogsmith uses Google Forms to receive expert contributions for articles.
- **CoSchedule's Headline Analyzer** (http://blgsmth.tips/coschedule): CoSchedule's tool for analyzing the effectiveness of headlines based on multiple factors.

- **Sharethrough's Headline Analyzer** (http://blgsmth.tips/sharethrough): Sharethrough's tool for analyzing the effectiveness of headlines, with actionable guidance to make improvements.
- **Advanced Marketing Institute Headline Analyzer** (http://blgsmth.tips/aminstitute): The Advanced Marketing Institute's tool for analyzing the effectiveness of headlines based on their emotional value.
- **Capitalize My Title** (http://blgsmth.tips/title-caps): A tool to convert titles to proper capitalization, based on your specified style.
- **Copyscape** (http://blgsmth.tips/copyscape): A plagiarism checking tool. The Blogsmith prefers it to Grammarly's plagiarism-checking tool, but both are helpful.
- **Nobias** (http://blgsmth.tips/nobias): A data-driven Chrome extension that helps detect and identify bias in news media.
- **Data.gov** (http://blgsmth.tips/data-gov): A searchable database of the US government's open data, which is helpful for gathering verifiable details about specific industries.
- **Statista** (http://blgsmth.tips/statista): A freemium database of authoritative and trustworthy statistics references. It's a great reference point for writers and editors looking to support claims.
- **Google Journalist Studio** (http://blgsmth.tips/journalist-studio): A free suite of tools for journalists that helps with all the details around reporting—gathering and displaying data, searching niche documents, and fact-checking.
- **The Weinstein Organization Chicago Power Words List** (http://blgsmth.tips/two-chicago): A useful reference list of power words to improve the strength of marketing messages.
- **Urban Dictionary** (http://blgsmth.tips/urban-dictionary): A dictionary for slang and other timely vernacular definitions.

- **Google Docs** (http://blgsmth.tips/google-docs): A user-friendly, collaborative word processing solution built in the cloud.
- **Notion** (http://blgsmth.tips/notion): A no-code platform for storing and organizing important information. The Blogsmith uses it as a company intranet.

Marketing/SEO Tools

- **Lumen5** (http://blgsmth.tips/lumen5): A tool for repurposing blog content as video. Its artificial intelligence (AI) functionality helps speed up the video editing process. Lumen5 videos are a great addition to social posts.
- **CloudApp** (http://blgsmth.tips/get-cloudapp): A screen recording and annotation tool that handles everything from screenshots to videos and GIFs. It helps quickly communicate ideas or direction.
- **Canva** (http://blgsmth.tips/canva): An approachable graphic design tool for creating simple visuals.
- **Design Pickle** (http://blgsmth.tips/designpickle): With expertise in creating ebooks and illustrations, Design Pickle is a graphic design service offering a minimum guaranteed daily queue of designs at a monthly flat rate.
- **Easelly** (http://blgsmth.tips/easelly): With expertise in creating infographics, Easelly is a graphic design service offering a minimum guaranteed daily queue of designs at a monthly flat rate.
- **Envato Elements** (http://blgsmth.tips/envato-elements): A subscription membership that includes access to various stock assets (video, photos, and audio), WordPress themes and plugins, as well as ebooks and course training material for a web designer audience. A subscription includes unlimited downloads for unlimited licenses across unlimited projects.

- **AppSumo** (http://blgsmth.tips/appsumo-home). A marketplace of lifetime software deals for an audience of entrepreneurs. It's a great place to grab a deal on early-stage tools while accepting the risk that some won't be supported forever. However, there's also the likelihood some will become more valuable to your business over time.
- **Depositphotos** (http://blgsmth.tips/depositphotos): A stock photo website with high-quality assets. It periodically runs deals on AppSumo.
- **Surfer** (http://blgsmth.tips/surfer): A suite of useful content search engine optimization (SEO) tools.
- **Moz's Title Tag Preview Tool** (http://blgsmth.tips/title-tool): A tool for previewing how meta titles would appear on the search engine results page (SERP).
- **Google Search Console** (http://blgsmth.tips/gsc): A free tool for analyzing your organic search performance and issues that may be negatively impacting it. It provides crucial reports around keyword rankings, technical and security errors, plus possible penalties to fix.
- **Keywords Everywhere** (http://blgsmth.tips/keywords-everywhere): A freemium Chrome and Firefox extension for uncovering keyword ideas based on the current SERP.
- **Keyword Surfer** (http://blgsmth.tips/keyword-surfer): Surfer's freemium Chrome extension for uncovering keyword ideas based on the current SERP.
- **Frase** (http://blgsmth.tips/frase): An AI content brief tool.
- **Clearscope** (http://blgsmth.tips/clearscope): An AI content optimization tool.
- **MarketMuse** (https://blgsmth.tips/marketmuse): An AI-powered content research tool.
- **Google Analytics** (http://blgsmth.tips/google-analytics): A straightforward, free web analytics platform. Install it and collect data to help inform business decisions.

- **Fathom Analytics** (http://blgsmth.tips/fathom): A privacy-focused web analytics platform that's comparable to Google Analytics.
- **Hotjar** (http://blgsmth.tips/hotjar): A freemium user feedback platform. By understanding how users interact with a brand's website, you can diagnose and fix any points of frustration.
- **Microsoft Clarity** (http://blgsmth.tips/microsoft-clarity): A free user behavior analytics tool, similar to Hotjar.
- **SerpWatch** (http://blgsmth.tips/serpwatch): A keyword rank tracking tool.
- **JotURL** (http://blgsmth.tips/joturl): A link shortening tool that offers the ability to add branded calls to action, use custom domains, and analyze results.
- **Sprout Social** (http://blgsmth.tips/sprout-social): A social media scheduling tool with many useful features, including a "social inbox" and data analysis to determine optimal posting times.
- **SleekBio** (http://blgsmth.tips/sleekbio): A link tree tool that expands social profile link limits to provide more than one clickable link.

Style Guides

- **New York University Social Media Style Guide** (http://blgsmth.tips/nyu): New York University's social media style guide. It contains useful specificity and examples that add context.
- **Sprout Social Seeds** (http://blgsmth.tips/sprout-style): Sprout Social's social media style guide. It's presented in a fun, branded visual format and shares a lot of guidance around expectations.
- **University of North Carolina Greensboro Social Media Style Guide** (http://blgsmth.tips/uncg): University of North Carolina Greensboro's social media style guide. It's short but

to the point—with examples of what works (and what doesn't), plus platform-specific guidelines.

- **Ask the Editors** (http://blgsmth.tips/ask-the-editors): *AP Stylebook* editors' weekly column about previously unresolved issues of style.
- **Mailchimp Content Style Guide** (http://blgsmth.tips/mailchimp-style): Mailchimp's brand style guide. It's well-rounded and about more than the written word.
- **Orbit Media Guest Blogging Guidelines** (http://blgsmth.tips/orbit-media): Orbit Media's brand style guide for facilitating blog guest contributions.
- **BuzzFeed Style Guide** (http://blgsmth.tips/buzzfeed): BuzzFeed brand style guide. It has great attention to detail and guidelines for timely news reporting.
- **A List Apart Style Guide** (http://blgsmth.tips/alistapart): A List Apart's brand style guide. It has useful guidance for articles that share code samples.
- **Google Developer Documentation Style Guide** (http://blgsmth.tips/google-developer): Google developers' brand style guide. It focuses on technical writing guidance.
- **Microsoft Writing Style Guide** (http://blgsmth.tips/microsoft-style): Microsoft's writing style guide. It has pointed guidance for communicating complex ideas in a simple manner.
- **Atlassian Design System** (http://blgsmth.tips/atlassian): Atlassian's style guide. It has guidance for being inclusive and writing according to the brand's voice and tone.

Recommended Books

- *The Elements of Style* (http://blgsmth.tips/elements):
  An essential guide to style.
- **Print version—***The Associated Press Stylebook*
  (http://blgsmth.tips/ap-stylebook): A reference guide for AP
  Style.
- **Digital access—***The Associated Press Stylebook*
  (http://blgsmth.tips/ap-digital): The digital version of the
  Associated Press Stylebook.
- **Google's Search Quality Rater Guidelines**
  (http://blgsmth.tips/google-qrg): Google's guidelines for
  human Quality Raters to determine if a web page meets the
  needs of users at a high enough level of quality.
- *The Adweek Copywriting Handbook*
  (http://blgsmth.tips/adweek): A guidebook and reference for
  effective copywriting principles.
- *On Writing* (http://blgsmth.tips/on-writing): Part Stephen
  King memoir, part writing guidebook.

Access Book Bonuses

Visit **www.writingforhumansandrobots.com/bonuses** for:

- A digital PDF copy of all Appendix resources.
- The Blogsmith Style Guide (short form version).
- The Blogsmith's social media style guide template.
- The Blogsmith's outline template.
- The Blogsmith's content brief template.
- Free access to my 1-hour Skillshare class, How to Write a Kick-
  Ass Blog Post.

ABOUT THE AUTHOR

MADDY OSMAN

M addy Osman is a digital native with a decade-long devotion to creating engaging, accessible, and relevant content. After teaching herself web design at age 11, she found her true passion in content creation—learning the intricacies while transitioning from technical to creative SEO marketer. Maddy's journey from freelance writer to founder and CEO of The Blogsmith yielded numerous insights to share about content creation for enterprise B2B technology brands. She believes in finding win-win situations for brands, readers, and robots—translated into actionable guidance throughout this book.

In *Writing for Humans and Robots*, Maddy gives a nod to editors and style mentors she's worked with at brands like Automattic, HubSpot, Adobe, Wix, and Trello. After benefitting from their thoughtful feedback, she has assembled this comprehensive guide to writing for the web in an attempt to pay it forward and create better quality content that's inclusive and accessible to readers.

Maddy has been recognized as one of **BuzzSumo's Top 100 Content Marketers** and **The Write Life's 100 Best Websites for Writers**. She has spoken for audiences at WordCamp US, SearchCon, and Denver Startup Week. When taking breaks from the digital world, Maddy enjoys cooking, reading, and exploring the world, but she is most content at home in Denver, Colorado, with her husband, Dan, and their pooch, Lola.

Keep up with Maddy's latest projects on Twitter: **@MaddyOsman**.

Printed in Great Britain
by Amazon